UNSOLVED LONDON MURDERS

TRUE CRIME FROM WHARNCLIFFE

Foul Deeds and Suspicious Deaths Series

Barking, Dagenham & Chadwell Heath
Barnsley
Bath
Bedford
Birmingham
Black Country
Blackburn and Hyndburn
Bolton
Bradford
Brighton
Bristol
Cambridge
Carlisle
Chesterfield
Colchester
Coventry
Croydon
Derby
Dublin
Durham
Ealing
Folkestone and Dover
Grimsby
Guernsey
Guildford
Halifax
Hampstead, Holborn and St Pancras
Huddersfield
Hull

Leeds
Leicester
Lewisham and Deptford
Liverpool
London's East End
London's West End
Manchester
Mansfield
More Foul Deeds Birmingham
More Foul Deeds Chesterfield
More Foul Deeds Wakefield
Newcastle
Newport
Norfolk
Northampton
Nottingham
Oxfordshire
Pontefract and Castleford
Portsmouth
Rotherham
Scunthorpe
Southend-on-Sea
Staffordshire and The Potteries
Stratford and South Warwickshire
Tees
Warwickshire
Wigan
York

OTHER TRUE CRIME BOOKS FROM WHARNCLIFFE

A-Z of Yorkshire Murder
Black Barnsley
Brighton Crime and Vice 1800-2000
Durham Executions
Essex Murders
Executions & Hangings in Newcastle
    and Morpeth
Norfolk Mayhem and Murder

Norwich Murders
Strangeways Hanged
The A-Z of London Murders
Unsolved Murders in Victorian and
    Edwardian London
Unsolved Norfolk Murders
Unsolved Yorkshire Murders
Yorkshire's Murderous Women

Please contact us via any of the methods below for more information or a catalogue.

WHARNCLIFFE BOOKS

47 Church Street – Barnsley – South Yorkshire – S70 2AS
Tel: 01226 734555 – 734222 Fax: 01226 – 734438
E-mail: enquiries@pen-and-sword.co.uk
Website: www.wharncliffebooks.co.uk

UNSOLVED LONDON MURDERS

MURDERS

The 1920s and 1930s

JONATHAN OATES

First published in Great Britain in 2009 by
Wharncliffe Books
an imprint of
Pen & Sword Books Ltd
47 Church Street
Barnsley
South Yorkshire
S70 2AS

Copyright © Jonathan Oates 2009

ISBN 978 1 84563 075 1

The right of Jonathan Oates to be identified as Author of this Work
has been asserted by him in accordance with the Copyright,
Designs and Patents Act 1988.

A CIP catalogue record for this book is available from the British
Library

Typeset in the UK by
Mac Style, Beverley, East Yorkshire

Printed and bound in the UK by
CPI

Pen & Sword Books Ltd incorporates the Imprints of Pen & Sword
Aviation, Pen & Sword Maritime, Pen & Sword Military,
Wharncliffe Local History, Pen and Sword Select, Pen and Sword
Military Classics and Leo Cooper.

For a complete list of Pen & Sword titles please contact
PEN & SWORD BOOKS LIMITED
47 Church Street, Barnsley, South Yorkshire, S70 2AS, England
E-mail: enquiries@pen-and-sword.co.uk
Website: www.pen-and-sword.co.uk

Contents

6

Acknowledgements

everal people have helped me with this book. John Coulter, Jane Kimber and James Marshall provided me with copies taken from local newspapers from Lewisham, Hammersmith and Hounslow Libraries. Paul Lang, John Coulter and Reg Eden allowed me to use a number of pictures from their collections of postcards and John Coulter took photographs for my use. William Bignell assisted me with his reminiscences of pre-war life in London.

More anonymously, I need to thank the staffs at the Westminster Archives Service, Kensington Library, the British Library, the British Library Newspaper Library and the National Archives, for providing microfilm, books, archives and electoral registers.

This book is dedicated to Jenny.

Introduction

Name a crime or criminal in the London of the 1920s and 1930s. I certainly couldn't, until I began writing about real crime in London a few years ago. Whereas, before then, even I could have named a Victorian killer (Jack the Ripper), an Edwardian one (Dr Crippen) or a post-war murderer (John Christie). For most people, crime in England in this period is dominated by the fictional whodunit. Conan Doyle's Sherlock Holmes stories still appeared in *The Strand* in the 1920s, though the stories were all set before 1914, and new sleuths, such as Agatha Christie's Hercule Poirot, Margery Allingham's Albert Campion and Dorothy L Sayers's Lord Peter Wimsey, all emerged in this era to do battle with fictional criminals, almost always taken from the middle and upper classes. Television and radio dramas and films have made these characters well known.

The real villains, their victims and their foul deeds have been largely overlooked, at least in the public mindset. Compendia of crime refer to some of these, such as the infamous case of Vera Page in 1931 and the Croydon poisonings of 1928–9, but most of these are now forgotten, and in any case, most have only been dealt with in a very cursory manner. The majority featured here have never been discussed in print since they were reported in the press. It is the aim of this book to bring them back to public view. This book deals with all the unsolved murders in

Ellie Norwood as Sherlock Holmes, 1920s.
Author's collection

London from the 1920s and 1930s. Among the crimes found here are a railway murder, the mystery of parts of a body found at Brentford and at Waterloo station, prostitute murders in Soho, the fatal shooting of a policeman, a brutal child murder and two IRA killings. It does not include the Croydon poisonings (1928–9), the murder of Louisa Steele (1931) or Robert Venner (1934), for though these are usually stated as being unsolved, the author's examination of police files has revealed that the police were well aware of who was responsible, but they lacked the evidence to bring the cases to trial. These two latter killings are detailed in the author's *Foul Deeds and Suspicious Deaths in Lewisham and Deptford*, and the police file on the Croydon case provides a convincing case against the killer who also escaped justice.

There is a mystery and a horror with unsolved murders. First, there is the horror of a brutal killing. Secondly, there is the mystery of who was responsible and the added horror of the knowledge that the killer walked free. They might have killed again. From the view of both police and friends and relations of the deceased, it is unfinished business, a chapter which can never be satisfactorily closed.

Birdhurst Rise, Croydon, 2007. © John Coulter.

The evidence for this book comes from a number of primary sources, documents written at the time of events or at least shortly afterwards. Most important are the murder files created by the investigating police officials themselves. These contain statements by witnesses, medical reports, anonymous letters, case summaries by the detectives and other related evidence. These are located at the National Archives at Kew. They give much more detail than that which appears in the press. Secondly, there are the newspaper reports of the time, which reveal the public facts as they emerged from police bulletins and reports of the inquests on the victims. *The Times* online was a principal source, but so too are local newspapers and the tabloid *Illustrated Police News*. Finally there are memoirs of serving officers, who discussed their cases, failures as well as successes. These give an insight into the thinking of the police, but should not always be taken as being entirely factual, as officers' memories are often at fault. I have also looked at books about crime, in order to learn what other writers have thought about these cases, though most have only given them a cursory survey.

Finally, a word about money in those pre-decimal times. Twelve pence (d.) made up one shilling (s.). Twenty shillings made up one pound (note). One pound and one shilling made up a guinea.

CHAPTER 1

The Police of London in the 1920s and 1930s

Seldom does one hear a good word for them.

Before we begin examining the crimes detailed in this book, we need first to take a glance at those whose job it was to investigate them, and discover their strengths and weaknesses. The bulk of the work fell onto the Metropolitan Police, founded in 1829 and reorganized in 1839. Their strength in 1933 was 20,154 and they were divided into 24 divisions, each covering part of London and Middlesex. They were of varying sizes and had differing numbers of police attached to each. For instance, Whitehall, division A, had an area of 1.88 square miles and a force of 694; whereas S division, Hampstead, was the largest with an area of 86.81 square miles and an establishment strength of 954. Each division was headed by a superintendent, who reported to the Chief Constable.

The numbers just quoted are 'establishment' figures and real numbers were usually below these; in 1923, by about 1,000. This meant that men had to undertake more than one beat per day and it made them more difficult to supervise. Despite the growth of the population of the metropolitan district between 1920 and 1940, there was no increase in police numbers.

The Metropolitan Police were under the command of the Police Commissioner, who answered to the Home Secretary, not to any directly elected body. Most commissioners were former military men who had no experience of police work and had little conception of the day-to-day lives of Londoners. Some were reluctant to take on the task, having had to be persuaded by the prime minister of the day to accept the role. Most were past their prime and some downright eccentric. Lord Byng, commissioner from 1928 to 1931, for example, refused to use a telephone or even have one in his office. Everyone else in the force had to work their way up from constable. George Cornish (1873–1959) began his 39 years service as a constable in the 1890s, and became a superintendent in the 1920s.

Almost all of the members of the police force were men. There had been the novelty of women police during the First World War (1914–18), but in 1922, in London, they numbered a mere 20; about 0.1 per cent of the whole. They had the power to make arrests, but were chiefly used in 'rescue work' among young women and girls. If they were out on patrol, they would always be followed by two male colleagues. Although it was felt that they were effective, in their limited remit, with Sir Leonard Dunning writing 'there is a definite place for women in the police force', the rank and file of the force were suspicious of them and hostile to any extension of their powers. One said that it was enough that married men were bossed about by their wife in the home; they had no desire for the like at work.

There had been major changes to the force towards the end of the First World War. For decades, the police had been very poorly paid; the job being seen as equivalent to that of an unskilled worker or an agricultural labourer, though it was far more dangerous and arduous. A National Union of Police had been formed and when a constable was dismissed in August 1918, the union called out the men on strike and about a third of the Metropolitan Police responded. The government responded in a conciliatory manner by reinstating the sacked man, and making improvements in pay and pensions. However, the union was not recognized and in the following year there was another strike in order to have the union officially recognized. This time, only a little over 1,000 men in London responded. Most did not want to jeopardize their recent gains. The strikers were all dismissed. In the same year, the Desborough Committee put forward a number of recommendations which were accepted by the government. These resulted in the formation of the Police Federation, a representative body for the men in the ranks up to the rank of inspector. It also made further increases in pay and pensions.

Policeman directs traffic in the City of London, 1920s. Paul Lang's collection

For some men, the pay rises resulted in a doubling or more of their wages. A constable's weekly wage rose from £1 10s to £3 10s. A police sergeant had an annual salary of £400 in 1928.

There were a number of ways in which technological changes were put into play as regards police work. The introduction of automatic traffic signals in 1931 relieved the police of the burden of having to control the ever increasing volume of motorized traffic. Each Metropolitan division had its own cars and vans for transport and supervisory work. Wireless communication between Scotland Yard and patrol cars was introduced in 1922. Police boxes became a familiar site in the main streets of London and proved to be a rapid method of communication, and each police station was now equipped with a telephone.

Other changes occurred. Lord Trenchard, Police Commissioner in the 1930s, founded the Hendon Police College, in order to promote and train men from the ranks to higher positions. This was treated with suspicion by radicals who claimed this would lead to the militarization of the force. A police laboratory was also set up at Hendon in 1934. A police driving school was also founded in that year. However, there was a tradition of conservatism and, as one assistant commissioner grudgingly noted, 'Modern preventative measures such as police boxes and the like are useful as far as they go.'

A leading figure in many murder investigations in the Metropolitan districts, and who features in most of the cases in this book, was Sir Bernard Spilsbury (1877–1947), a Home Office pathologist. He was usually on hand to identify the causes of death of murder victims and to carry out post mortems. He had first come to prominence in the public eye in 1912 when he was involved in the Dr Crippen murder case. He also gave evidence, usually for the prosecution, during murder trials and such was his repute that his words carried great weight among juries. However, more recently his ability has come into question, and it seems certain that his testimony in the case of Donald Merritt in 1926, where the verdict of not proven was brought against a young man who almost certainly shot his mother dead, was erroneous. The accused man later went on to commit a double murder.

Most policemen patrolled on foot. The daily beat began at 5.45 am. There would be a parade and instructions at the

Scotland Yard. John Coulter's collection

police station. Then the men would file off, under their sergeants, until each man had begun his beat. This beat lasted from 6 am to 2 pm. The rest of the day was divided into two other beats of equal length.

The detailed detection of crime rested with the Criminal Investigation Department (CID). These plain-clothed detectives, not the divisional police, investigated the murders discussed in this book, though they were expected to report their findings to the divisional superintendent. The CID was recruited from the uniformed service. Any new recruit to the detective service had to pass exams and show proof of his superior powers of observation.

Apart from the Met, there were a number of other police forces in the capital. One was the City of London Police. This was controlled by the City of London, not the government. Its headquarters were in Old Jewry and had a strength of just over 1,000 men. There was also the River Police, which was part of the Met, and its officers patrolled in motor boats. Finally, there was the railway police, maintained by the railway companies. The Southern Railway Company ran the railways in the south of England and their police were involved in the detection of crime on the railways around London, as noted in Chapter 9.

The police were far from perfect. Even a writer in 1934 who was sympathetic to the force had to admit, 'there have been black sheep – and there may be still – in the ranks of the police as there are in every other section of the community'. There was public shock when it was revealed in 1928 that one PS Goddard at Vine Street police station, had been amassing a fortune in bribes from nightclub and brothel owners, which enabled him to buy a large house and a fast car, as well as to accumulate over £17,000 in cash. He was sacked and spent three years in jail.

Low-level corruption was more common, at least judging from anecdotal evidence. Nightclub owners, bookmakers, prostitutes and publicans all gave bribes in order that police would turn a blind eye to their semi-legal status or assist if they were in trouble with criminals. Some of this might only have been low level, with one superintendent stating that the habit of publicans leaving beer for the beat constable was 'simply a token of genuine friendship'. Another example of corruption was noted by 'Boy' Mulcaster in *Brideshead Revisited*, when he and his friends are stopped by the police in London: 'There's no need for you to notice anything. We've just come from Ma Mayfield's. I reckon she pays you a nice retainer to keep your eyes shut. Well, you can keep 'em shut on us too, and you won't be the losers by it.' Later, when Rex Mottram comes to their aid after their arrest, 'with the slightest nuance, he opened the way for bribery' and gives the desk sergeant a havana cigar. However, in both these instances, the police do not accept bribes, though clearly it was envisaged that they would. Tipping was a recognized element in a policeman's renumeration, even to the extent of helping the rich in and out of their cars. Yet corruption may have been at a lesser level after Trenchard became commissioner in 1931. Nor was it prevalent. When two constables found a middle-aged man with a younger woman in Hyde Park, they planned to have them charged with public indecency. The man tried to bribe them, but they withstood the temptation. He turned out to be Sir Basil Thompson, once Assistant Commissioner at Scotland Yard.

The police in London had not only to deal with criminals in the inter-war period, but were also involved in political disputes. There were fears about Bolshevism among the working classes in the 1920s and, on one occasion, a procession of the unemployed was dispersed by a baton charge on the grounds that most of them were 'low class' Jews, and therefore suspected as being Bolsheviks. The principal crisis in the 1920s, though, was the General Strike of 1926, when the police had to ensure that food supplies got through and that the volunteers running the transport system were unmolested. This sometimes involved them in clashes with the strikers. Evelyn Waugh noted that the police had to disperse a crowd in Hammersmith by a baton charge and a similar method of crowd dispersal was used in Southall. The police were also on the receiving end of violence in Hanwell, where some men threw stones at them. In *Brideshead Revisited*, during the Strike, a policeman is knocked to the ground and is being kicked by half a dozen youths, and another has a head injury during a disturbance in the Commercial Road.

In the 1930s, the threat to public order came from the far right. The formation of the British Union of Fascists by Sir Oswald Mosley led to violence between groups of political extremists. Although the police did not sympathize with Mosley's socialist opponents, they did not approve of the Blackshirts trying to impose their own form of order on the streets. Matters came to a head in 1936 when Mosley planned a march through the Jewish districts of the East End. This led to the 'Battle of Cable Street', where the police clashed with crowds who opposed such a provocative gesture.

In both instances, the police earned the enmity of sections of the London community. They were not seen as impartial upholders of the law but, certainly by some, as enemies of the working class. One observer noted 'the curious fact that a crowd, particularly in working class districts, is almost invariably hostile to the police'. A priest remarked, 'seldom does one hear a good word for them'. Notting Dale was a notoriously rough part of London. In 1929, following the arrest of a suspect, there were verbal and physical attacks on the police and the police had to barricade the police station on occasion. Neal's Yard in Monmouth Street, Covent Garden, was a place, in the words of a veteran policeman, 'where [thugs] break all you young coppers in'. There had been fighting between police and people on Peace Night in 1919 and one observer said 'I have never seen in all my life such a hostile crowd'. In 1923, there were 1,429 cases of injuries to police officers. Part of this animosity was because there were instances of the police beating up suspects and planting evidence on them. Sometimes policemen misused their powers and in 1928 one Helen Adele was falsely accused because she would not have sex with two constables. Mr William Bignell recalled troublemakers at the Tottenham National Assistance offices in the 1950s and an ex-copper told him that in the 'old days', i.e. before 1939, the police would simply have taken the offender behind the premises and seen to it that he would not repeat his offence. Despite this, senior officers tried to create a more favourable image. Thomas

Divall wrote 'I can assure the public that the "bobby" is a real good fellow, and if they would only treat and trust him as such, there will be a much better feeling between the two.'

Although the middle classes were generally supportive of the police – Agatha Christie's Hercule Poirot refers to them as 'a brave and intelligent force of men' – they had reason to be in conflict with the police too. First, they were shocked by scandals such as the Goddard case and other police misdemeanours which were made public in this era, such as the wrongful arrest and failed prosecution of innocent people. Secondly, the increased use of motor cars meant that they came into conflict with the law enforcers. However, middle-class volunteers cooperated with the police during the General Strike, to their mutual benefit and appreciation.

Relations with the press were often poor, too. Superintendent Percy Savage wrote of 'the lack of efficient co-operation between the police and the public. It is indeed a strange and regrettable fact that there is – and always has been – a strong disinclination in certain police circles to take the public fully and frankly into their confidence.'

The Metropolitan Police force undoubtedly had its defects in the inter-war period. How far these examples of misbehaviour were commonplace is difficult to discern, however. Their popularity and the trust they were held in, or not, were clearly important for solving crime. Yet as we shall see in the next chapter, they did have a fair amount of success.

CHAPTER 2

Crime in London between the World Wars

All great cities are magnets for crooks, gamblers, dope pedlars, prostitutes, pimps and perverts and riff raff of all kinds.

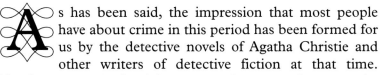s has been said, the impression that most people have about crime in this period has been formed for us by the detective novels of Agatha Christie and other writers of detective fiction at that time. Murders are committed in country houses and among the upper middle classes. They are solved by private detectives. This, however, is fiction. We must now look at the facts.

Criminality in London was always a diverse affair and this period was no exception. While the Chicago gangsters of this era are well known, there were also criminal gangs in London. The most famous were the Sicilian gangster clan, the Sabinis. They committed burglaries, thefts, extorted money from prostitutes and book keepers, and fought rival gangs. They mostly used knives and razors to settle disputes over protection rackets. There were also shoot outs, with Henry Sabini being shot dead in Great Bath Street in 1922. They also fought with other gangs both in London and outside. Charabancs would take the fighters from Saffron Hill, the famous Italian quarter just to the west of the City, and Stepney, to the race courses of Greenford and Epsom Downs. Or there could be violence and intimidation in London races, such as at Alexandra Palace in 1921. Common battle grounds were Holborn, Clerkenwell and Gray's Inn Road.

At first the police did little (some policemen even connived and protected these gangsters), though in part this was because few would testify against the gangsters. Yet in 1922, 60 policemen arrested 100 of the criminals. The Sabinis were not finally defeated until they were interned as enemy aliens in

1940, but their activities had been curtailed from about 1930, with Inspector Hambrooke remarking that Scotland Yard could 'predict with confidence that the terrorist days of the gangsters as we have known them are gone, never to return'. Another foreign gang were the Messinas, also from Italy, who founded a vice empire in Soho of gambling dens and brothels, using both British and Italian girls in the latter. Soho in the 1920s was the centre of the cocaine trade in London.

Most crime, however, was the work of individuals. The 1927 *London Guide* warned visitors to the capital of the dangers of crime. 'A favourite dodge of the light fingered fraternity is to join a crowd for one of the motor omnibuses. Standing on the steps as if about to enter, they work their will while the scrimmage for buses ensue, and then hastily alight.' In public places, especially on vehicles, the poster 'Beware of pickpockets' was a common sight. Thieves often carried overcoats over their arms to use as a screen for their nefarious activities.

Crime was not dominated by foreign gangs, despite their demonization in the press. As Chief Constable Frederick Wensley wrote, 'The cleverest thieves … are undoubtedly born cockneys'. Crime was usually the province of the poor.

Dockers, with their weekly pay packets, were a common target for pickpockets and in 1927 nine Shoreditch pickpockets were apprehended en route to Poplar and Canning Town. Groups of women from Hoxton often took part in shoplifting expeditions, reselling the goods at markets. Poor people valued their padlocks in order to safeguard their few possessions and in some districts it was unsafe to hang the washing outside if one was absent from home.

Comic policeman: few people saw the guardians of law in this light. Author's collection

Cars were increasingly used in crimes. Basil Thompson wrote 'the motor car has served the criminal far more than it has the police'. Smash and grab motor bandits targeted jewellers and Ruby Sparks from Camberwell was particularly notorious in this field in the 1920s. Car theft and resale was another burgeoning industry. A Brixton gang specialized in stealing from garages in Camberwell and the Oval. New number plates were useful and a crooked clerk in the London County Council proved helpful here.

Burglary was another offence, both of shops and houses, in this era. The first cat burglar on Park Lane was one Gussie Delaney in 1924. In the following decade, burglars used flexible plastic to overcome Yale locks. Houses in Golders Green and Hampstead were particularly targeted from the late 1920s.

Despite all this, generally speaking, crime was at a low level, though contemporaries, unaware of the higher crime rates that would follow the Second World War, were concerned. After all, as a source noted, 'a large proportion of the offences committed in the United Kingdom take place within the borders of London'. In the 1930s, recorded crime was on the increase, though only about a hundred every year included violence. We shall now examine some figures. In 1913, there had been 7,000 trials for assault and only 4,500 in 1939. Drunkenness cases fell from a pre-war level of 70,000 to 18,000. Whereas in 1903 there had been 553 recorded burglaries, in 1928 there were 473. Larcenies were almost halved to 1,135. Wensley wrote 'Indiscriminate violence has, in fact, gone out of fashion with the criminal classes.' Yet, although the London of the 1930s was safer than that before 1914, there was an overall increase in recorded crime in London from 1934 to 1939 of 13.4 per cent, from 83,700 offences to 94,900. However, by the standards of later years this was low, with 570,000 offences in 1978 (when the capital's population was lower than in the 1930s). It was thus nonsense for a modern Home Secretary to state in 2008 that London has never been safer than at present.

There were hotbeds of crime in the capital and Campbell Street in Islington was thought to be the worst street in

London. Policemen, children and strangers avoided it if at all possible, though its inhabitants chiefly stole from one another. This was a very poor neighbourhood, it was criminal and overcrowded. Theft, violence and gambling were commonplace and in a typical year in the 1920s a dozen of its residents would be in prison. Yet by the 1930s, even this street became more law abiding, with increased policing and the exodus of some of its residents.

Many Londoners had no first-hand experience of crime, nor much fear of it. Mr Bignell recalls that his parents, who lived in Hornsey in the 1930s, had no fears about crime, and his mother often went out late at night, and alone, in order to do her shopping, walking through darkened streets. How common this experience was is another question, however. Yet London diarists at this time also indicate that crime and the fear of crime was low, if not non-existent. Evelyn Waugh's only brush with the law was in 1925 when he spent the night in a police cell for drunkenness; he was never the victim of crime. Nor was Henry St John, a civil servant who lived in west London in the 1920s and 1930s. Mr A K Goodlet did record being attacked in Ealing in 1934 by some roughs, but that was the only time he experienced crime and he seems to have quickly forgotten it.

Murder, too, was at a relatively low level in these years. Wensley wrote 'Murder investigations, so far as Scotland Yard is concerned, happen much more frequently in books than in real life.' This is despite the fact that greater London's population rose throughout these decades from 7.5 million in 1921 to about 8.6 million people in 1939, the largest number that had ever lived there, before or since. Between 1921 and 1939, there were 490 murders in London (and of these, more than 95 per cent were cleared up). This compares very favourably with the numbers of fatal crimes in the early twenty-first century, which numbered 475 in 2004–6. We should also remember that the number of murders in the inter-war years was inflated by cases of women dying as a result of abortions and the fact that some of victims would have survived in more recent years because of advances in medicine. Furthermore, there were a large number of weapons

London at night. Paul Lang's collection

in private hands following the First World War and many young men who knew how to use them. Finally, people were poorer in this period compared to the later twentieth century: clearly the link between poverty and crime is a tenuous one. Londoners were far more likely to be killed in road accidents in London (these averaged 1,000 per annum in the 1920s and 1,400 per year in the 1930s) and violence against the person was very rare. Quite why these decades were so safe is another question, but that it was so is undoubted. One possible explanation was offered in 1932, 'Observers at home and abroad, whatever their views on capital punishment, agree that the stringent deterrent is the certainty of being found out.' It must be noted that many convicted killers were given jail sentences, rather than being hanged.

Unsolved murders were rare, despite Sir Charles Cayzer, MP for Chester, referring in 1932, to 'the large number of unsolved murder cases in the last two years'. More accurately, in the Agatha Christie book, *The Thirteen Problems*, published in the same year, the following discussion occurs:

'Are there a lot of crimes that go unpunished, or are they not?'

'You're thinking of newspaper headlines, Mrs Bantry. SCOTLAND YARD AT FAULT AGAIN. And a list of unsolved mysteries to follow'.

'Which really, I suppose, form a very small percentage of the whole?'

'Yes, that is so'.

Even in the case of unsolved murders (about 5 per cent of the total),

> it does not necessarily follow, that, because a murder is classed as undiscovered, the police do not know who committed the crime. In many cases the explanation is that some vital link in the chain of evidence is missing, and from circumstances beyond the control of the police it cannot be obtained.

On the other hand, as Wensley wrote, some may have gone unreported:

> It was not in those days a very extraordinary thing for a dead body to be found in the street during the night or in the early hours, and it was significant that this usually occurred not far from houses to which all sorts of bad characters were known to resort. Few of these cases were classed officially as murder . . . but that there had been foul play was often very likely.

He added that murder investigations were 'either very simple or very difficult to handle'. If victim and criminal knew each other, as many did, or if the criminal confessed at once, which was not uncommon, matters were fairly straightforward. If it was a case of murder by a stranger, whether for money or due to lust, then enquiries were far more difficult. Chief Inspector Arthur Neil absolved the force from failure, and wrote that 'I am certain the fault do not lie with the police.'

London was the largest city in the world and contained about a fifth of England's population. As Chief Superintendent Thorp wrote, 'All great cities are magnets for crooks, gamblers, dope pedlars, prostitutes, pimps and perverts and general riff raff' and London was no exception. We shall now investigate some of their deeds.

CHAPTER 3

Death in Chelsea, 1920

he read Buxton's hand and told her that she would meet a violent end – and now she is murdered

M rs Frances Buxton, aged 53, was the landlady of the Cross Keys pub on Lawrence Street, Chelsea. She had been married to one Frank Charles Buxton in Toronto, Canada, in 1888, and they had had at least one married daughter by 1920. This was Mrs Gwendolin Wehrle of Phene Street, also in Chelsea. In about 1908, Frances had separated from her husband. This was due to his dislike of her political views (she favoured the suffragettes and, worse still, socialism) and also because he had had an affair in America and passed a venereal disease onto her. She did not see him again until August 1919 and at this time, he was the landlord of the Sussex Hall, Sidley, at Bexhill on Sea. He never saw her again. Mrs Buxton had been the licensee of at least

Chelsea Bridge. Author's collection

three pubs; the old George at Kensington, the Star at Isleworth and, since 1914, the Cross Keys. When she was at the Star, she took on a partner, a younger man called Arthur Cutting, and he was her partner at the Cross Keys, too. This was not an unmixed blessing. One Henry John Penn, of Stern Street, Shepherd's Bush, a ball finisher's assistant and an old friend of Mrs Buxton (since at least 1910), recalled, 'I remember on one occasion Mrs Buxton came to my place at Shepherd's Bush and asked me to come over and stay the night at her house to protect her, as this Mr Cutting had attacked her and held her down.' We shall hear more of Cutting later.

The Cross Keys was a brick-built beer house about 50 yards from the Chelsea Embankment. It was three storeys high and had a broad frontage, being described as a 'large gloomy building of the early Georgian period'. At the front of the house was a large public bar, which would have been mainly patronized by men. At the back was the saloon and private bar, where women and men mixed more freely. Mrs Buxton slept alone in the house, on the second floor. She employed two women as barmaids: Mrs Mitchell and her daughter, Lily Mitchell, who also worked in a jewellery shop. There was a potman, one Henry Whitehead, who was about 60. For company, she had a little Pomeranian dog.

PC George Hammond had passed the pub twice late on Saturday night, 17 January 1920, and found the doors were locked, though there was a light burning inside somewhere. Checking whether premises were locked was a major part of the night beat at this time, and continued to be so until at least the 1960s. On Sunday morning, at 12.35, his replacement on the beat, PC Leslie Betts, visited the pub, again, presumably to check that the premises were secure, rather than to have a drink, and found that the door to the saloon bar, at the side of the pub and through an archway, was open. He later made the following statement:

> I went in and found the place smothered with smoke inside. I blew my whistle, and went straight upstairs and looked in all the rooms. I could find none, so I came down again and

looked over the house, and found smoke was coming from the cellar. Curtains were drawn across the top of the cellar doors. I tried to go down, but I was driven back by the smoke.

He then summoned the fire brigade by going to the nearest fire alarm, which was close to Chelsea old church. Station Officer Mr C J Brown, of the Brompton Fire Station, Chelsea, received a call at a quarter to one that morning. He and his men arrived on the scene. They went down to the cellar and extinguished the flames with ease. Brown recalled what happened next:

I went down to the cellar. In the back cellar and basement, the door was open and I saw a heap of what appeared to be sacking or rubbish in front of me. The light was bad, but when I examined the heap I found it to be a body. There was a quantity of sawdust, two bundles of bedding, some siphons of soda water and some odds and ends.

The upper portion of the body was covered in sawdust and the other part partially so. At the foot of the body was a shovel and there was also some sacking under the corpse's legs. Although the sacking had been on fire, the sawdust was not. He found traces of a silk dress and white underclothing. The body was one of a fully clothed woman. Her head and face were battered and covered with blood. Brown called to Betts that he had found someone who was almost dead and that he should try and find a doctor. Betts did so, and brought Dr Grosvenor back with him, who lived at Ogle Street, Chelsea, and was the police surgeon for the division. They arrived at the pub shortly after one.

Betts recalled the changed scene:

To my surprise, I saw a woman lying on the floor [*he had thought the firemen said that it was a man's body, but Brown denied this*] in the saloon bar. She had been carried up by the firemen, who were trying artificial respiration. I saw that she had been knocked about the head.

The landlady's dog was running around the bar and was quite lively. It did not bark at the constable. In the mean time, the doctor was examining the body, which was of Mrs Buxton, and he pronounced that life was extinct. He thought that she had died less than an hour before, namely some time after midnight. The body was still warm, though the hands were

The Cross Keys pub, 2008. Author's collection

cold. He was shown a broken bottle and a pool of blood in the cellar where she had been found and concluded that she might well have been killed by the bottle. The wounds included slashes on both cheeks, several to the back of the head, one to the nose, and also slight burns on the calf of the left leg. She had been dead before the sawdust was set alight.

Police made initial enquiries, questioning various men and talking to Frank Buxton, but none could help. Details of another man whom they sought were issued. He was tall, dark and wore an overcoat and a soft felt hat, and had been in the pub on the night of the murder. None of the neighbours heard or saw anything suspicious.

Mrs Buxton probably ate after closing the pub, as the remains of a meal were found. She had not gone to bed; it had not been slept in. Her dog did not seem unduly alarmed, which was seen as significant, as it had a shrill bark, yet had raised no outcry. Her black cat did nothing, either.

Mrs Barford, who lived in the tenement buildings opposite the pub, was one of the last to leave and recalled that all in the pub were regulars. Two men were playing dominoes. She thought that the landlady 'seemed in the best of spirits'. She said that Mrs Buxton was popular but was not very communicative. Her pub had been burgled recently and she had allegedly purchased a revolver as a precaution.

The inquest was held on 20 January at the offices of the Chelsea Board of Guardians. Mr H R Oswald was the coroner for the Western District of London and he presided. Superintendent Carlin and Inspector Burton represented the police. There were also men there to represent the brewery who owned the house, Messrs Barclay, Perkins & Co.

The estranged husband of the deceased gave his limited evidence about the couple's history as previously described. PC Betts and Mr Brown followed with their testimonies. Mrs Mitchell, the wife of a jeweller, was one of the barmaids and had been working on the Saturday evening. She and her daughter had helped to wipe the glasses and tidy up after ten o'clock, before leaving at about half past ten. She recalled that Mrs Buxton was the only one in the pub when she left, 'She was quite alone. She stood in the doorway leading to the saloon bar from the parlour [near to the stairs leading to the cellar] as we were leaving and said to us, "Good-night. God bless you'".

Mrs Mitchell thought that the pub had been busy that night. Takings had been as much as between £18 and £20. The takings were put into a little basket after they had been through the till and Mrs Buxton then took these upstairs to her bedroom. Usually £6 in change was left in the till. Mrs Mitchell also mentioned that Mrs Buxton often wore jewellery in the bar, and on that evening wore a diamond crescent brooch on her breast and a diamond star above. She also wore a gold curved bracelet, a wedding ring, a keeper ring and a single stone diamond ring.

She was then asked about a number of named individuals. Mrs Mitchell said that Whitehead had left at nine that Saturday night and had not returned. She knew nothing of Cutting. She said that Penn, who had occasionally been employed at the pub, had not been there for about a month or six weeks, because she had done bar work and so he was not needed. He was not there that Saturday.

Lily Mitchell was the next to speak. She had been working there from a quarter to nine, but had been sitting in the saloon bar as a customer up to ten o'clock. She remembered a man coming to the pub just before ten, when the bar was otherwise empty. When asked to describe him she said, 'He had a cap well down on his face. He was tall and his cap was a peaked cap of fairly light grey cloth. He was wearing something dark.' Apparently he ordered a pint of bitter and Mrs Buxton served him. He was fairly well dressed and slightly grey haired. She was unsure whether she would recognize him again, and said that he might have been able to have concealed himself in the pub, probably the cellar, without being seen, for he was by himself for at least ten minutes.

Whitehead made the brief comment that he had been there on the Saturday, doing some odd jobs for Mrs Buxton. He had checked the cellar before he left at nine and had found that nothing was out of order.

Contrary to what Mrs Mitchell had said, Penn declared that he had been in the pub on the Thursday afternoon preceding the murder. On being asked if he had seen any strange customers, he answered readily. He had seen a tall man in the private bar. This character was about five feet ten or eleven inches. He was wearing a brown coat and a blue suit. He was in his mid-thirties, but Penn could not recall whether he was wearing a cap or a bowler (in this period men almost always wore headgear, unless they were very eccentric). The man's hair was not grey, but he had a fair moustache, was dark-eyed and had a very long face. This sounds like a younger man than the one described by Lily. Penn had never seen him before or since and said that he was not a regular. Apparently the man was sitting at the back and was moving about, looking at the landlady's jewellery, which she wore as usual in a conspicuous manner. Whitehead thought 'there was something funny about him' and that he had eyes for Mrs Buxton only.

Apparently, when the pub closed for the afternoon, Whitehead stayed behind with Mrs Buxton and he referred to the stranger, in a jocular fashion.

'I see there was someone in the bar trying to give you the glad eye.'

'Yes. That man has been in the house three or four days, and he had been foxing me. I have got him set.'

He had left the pub at half past six, after putting the lights on for her. He thought that Mrs Buxton had the habit of keeping a lot of money on the premises and only banking it when she had amassed a great deal.

Another guest at the pub on the fatal Saturday was Mrs Wehrle, arriving between half past eight and a quarter to nine and leaving alone at ten. She, too, saw a man in the saloon bar whom she had not seen before. Her description of him was similar to Lily's and her comments about him were also similar. However, she thought that her mother might have been acquainted with him. She thought the man spoke like a Londoner and was well educated. She had also seen two men in the bar together about half an hour earlier, one of whom was rather drunk and had asked for two double whiskies. The first man seemed to be of a better class than his drunken friend, and had a pale, thin face with protruding eyes and wore a cap and overcoat. His companion was broad, tall and stout, with a fat face and a thick neck. Both left the premises before ten. These two men were James Ballardie, a 40-year-old director, and James Bell, a clerk. It was verified that both men went home after leaving the pub.

Finally, there was the medical evidence. Although Dr Grosvenor had been the first doctor on the scene, it had fallen to Dr Reginald Robert Ellworthy to conduct the post mortem, which he had done on the Monday after the murder. He said that there were many marks of extreme violence on the face and there was a piece of coloured glass in one of these. Apart from the blows by a bottle, the nose had been damaged by a fist and there were also indications of strangulation. 'It struck me that it was done by a thin cord of a tough nature'. The doctor added: 'A lot of unnecessary violence was used to make sure' that the woman was dead. Yet the cause of death was heart failure due to shock and concussion due to the blows to the head, and this had been accelerated by the strangulation.

The inquest was adjourned until 3 February. Yet no one was ever charged with the crime. The witnesses suggested that the

Glebe Place, once home of Charles Rennie Mackintosh, 2008. Author's collection

man in the saloon bar may have been responsible. Could he have been an opportunist thief, who had heard of Mrs Buxton's money and jewellery? Or was it someone else?

Mrs Buxton had had several men in her life. Perhaps the most surprising of all was the following. Charles Rennie Mackintosh (1868–1927), the famous Scottish architect and artist, was one. He lived in Glebe Place, Chelsea, from 1915 to 1921 (this street leads south to Lawrence Street) and had borrowed money from Mrs Buxton on several occasions – he owed her £7 10s at the time of her death. Mackintosh first became acquainted with Mrs Buxton in about 1915. Furthermore, when his wife (Margaret MacDonald, a fellow artist) was away in July 1917, he had had a brief affair with her. He also had a key to the saloon bar at one time, but said he had returned it. However, his name was kept from the public and he does not seem to have been a likely suspect. The police checked his movements on the night of the murder and he had an alibi.

Buxton himself was a suspect, as he resembled one of the strangers seen at the pub, but his movements that night were checked and he was cleared. As Penn was the sole beneficiary of her will, to the extent of £1,436 8s, he was a suspect, but as the police report stated:

Having ascertained that Penn was practically the only person who would benefit by the death of Mrs Buxton, thorough investigation was made into his movements during the week preceding Saturday 17 January and particularly upon that day and night, but we confirmed his statement in every detail.

Arthur Cutting had lived with Mrs Buxton for eight months during the recent war, before joining the army. She was known to be afraid of him and Mackintosh testified that this was true. During their liaison, they had quarrelled and hit each other, and were often drunk. Cutting claimed not to have seen her for three years, 'I can assure you I have not been in Chelsea for some three years.' But George Thurgood and one Miss Thompson independently claimed to have seen him with two other men in the vicinity of the pub three weeks before. Cutting claimed that on the night of the murder he had been with his girlfriend, Miss Bella Dick, and her family in Shepherd's Bush and these people corroborated this. Nor could he have been seen by the two witnesses, for he had been at work each day in January and for most of December, save for the brief Christmas holiday. This was confirmed by his boss, Mr Lacey, 'a highly respectable man', and he had work timesheets to prove it. Even the police were convinced. 'Enquiries were at once made by careful officers and the whole of the persons mentioned by Cutting were seen. They all corroborated his story and as we had absolutely no evidence against him, he was allowed to go.'

A more mysterious figure was Mr E F Walker, who was lodging in Kennington. He had left there on the Saturday evening of the murder and returned the following morning. He was in his thirties and was a tall man. He was never traced. Yet there was no direct proof that he was the killer, or that he was ever even at the pub at any time.

A number of other suspects also emerged. William Welling pointed the finger at one Joseph Dixon, a 33 year old employed at the Ministry of Pensions. Apparently, Welling's girlfriend, one Miss Gwennie Gadd, told him 'It's funny, Dick (Dixon) told me that he read Buxton's hand and told her she would meet with a violent end – now she is murdered.' She added that 'I am afraid of that man Dick'. On enquiry, the police found there was 'not a tittle of evidence' against Dixon and, furthermore, Miss Gadd was an unreliable witness, being 'of intemperate habits'. Finally, none of the witnesses identified Dixon as the man they had seen in the pub.

William Lawton, an assistant cook on board the SS *Valencia*, thought that a fellow cook, George Lux, a man in his forties, was suspect. He told the police, 'I thought by Lux's actions and the way he behaved that he might know something about the affair'. Lux appeared shifty and had been doing a lot of washing before the ship left London. He also mentioned the murder. Yet none of the witnesses identified Lux.

Arthur Stephens was in the Duke of York pub near Victoria railway station and heard four men have a suspicious conversation. They were discussing the murder and when they noticed Stephens was taking an interest, one said, 'Don't say too much, take care, he might be a detective'. One pulled off his glove and revealed a bandaged hand. One of his companions remarked, 'Yes, and I would murder someone myself if I thought they had the means and I hadn't.' One of the others then remarked, 'We had better clear off' and so they did. Stephens recalled that one was wearing a Canadian army uniform.

In 1922, Polly Wilson of Forest Gate named Charles Clay, a railway employee, as being guilty of the crime, claiming that he and Emily Higgins, the woman he lived with, had some of the jewellery taken from Mrs Buxton. Clay was questioned and he did indeed recall the murder and said that Mrs Buxton was his cousin's wife, though he had not seen her for 16 years. He attended the inquest, but denied murder. Although he resembled a suspect, he was found to be at work at the time of the murder. Detective Inspector Hedley concluded that 'no evidence whatever had been obtained which would show that Clay was in any way connected with the murder of Mrs Buxton'.

Five years later, Netley Lucas, a writer, contacted the police on behalf of John Francis O'Connor. The latter had recently been released from prison on the Continent. He was from Liverpool and was a thief who told Lucas that he had killed Mrs Buxton. There was some press coverage of this, but it was found to be a hoax, though whether Lucas was O'Connor's dupe or his confederate was never ascertained. Lucas (born in 1904) was a fraudster and confidence trickster. He had been in trouble with the law since his early teens and was to be sentenced in 1932 to 18 months hard labour for fraud, so this was probably yet another of his money-making schemes.

The final communication on this matter came in the form of an anonymous letter of 14 April 1932, which was sent from New York to the Commissioner, Viscount Byng, and read as follows:

The man who killed Mrs Frances Buxton in January 1920 of the Cross Keys Inn on Laurence Street, Chelsea is Edward Cooney ex convict of Brooklyn, New York, when you arrest him I will testify against him not before.

Your servant,
One Hoo Knows.

Edward Cooney, an American, had indeed been in a New York prison until 1931, but his present whereabouts could not be ascertained.

If the killer could not be identified, was the motive clear? It may have been robbery, as money and possibly jewellery was missing. Yet Dr Grosvenor claimed, 'A lot of unnecessary violence was used when she was dying.' And the police concluded, 'After the most exhaustive investigation we have failed to obtain a tittle of evidence against any particular person. We feel inclined to believe that the motive for this crime may have been more than robbery.' They thought it may have been revenge. Mrs Buxton had suffered from venereal disease and may have passed this on to one of the men she had been intimate with, though all those who we know of were cleared; perhaps there was another man. As Detective Inspector Alfred Burton concluded, 'it is quite possible that one of them may have committed this offence for revenge'.

Whatever his motive and whoever he was, he escaped detection completely.

CHAPTER 4

The Murder of a Policeman, 1921

*I saw a man who was acting suspiciously. I made a run for him
and he fired three times and I fell down.*

Gunnersbury Lane in south east Ealing had been a
notorious haunt of highwaymen in the eighteenth
century. A prime minister had been robbed there
and it was here that Sixteen String Jack made his
last heist in 1774 (chronicled in the author's *Foul Deeds and
Suspicious Deaths in Ealing*). It was still a dangerous place in
the early twentieth century. One reason for this was the
potentially rich pickings to be found in the locality. To the
south of Gunnersbury Lane was Gunnersbury Park, which
since the 1830s had been a country estate of 186 acres which
was owned by the wealthy banking family, the Rothschilds,
and in 1921 was home to the widowed Mrs Leopold
Rothschild (Marie Perugia, 1863–1937). They also owned
most of the land in the district too.

In the early hours of Wednesday 11 February, PC James
Kelly of T division was on his beat, which extended along
Gunnersbury Lane, from the Ealing end, as far as Acton Town
underground station, which was on the District line. This part
of Gunnersbury Lane was hardly built up at all, and consisted
mainly of playing fields adjoining the road. There were also a
few large houses; the so-called Manor House, rented by a Mr
Leyman, who was then in Switzerland, and Gunnersbury
Lodge, both of which were north of the road. To the south of
the road was the Rothschild estate as mentioned above.

PC Kelly was 34 years old and resided on Elliott Road,
Chiswick. Until recently he had lived and worked in south
London. He had married in January 1921. At 9.45 pm,
Inspector Williams of Chiswick had paraded the constables
ready for the night beat. These included Kelly, who was
assigned to the Gunnersbury Lane beat. The inspector then

Gunnersbury Park, 1930s. Paul Lang's collection

saw him at 10.40 near Thorneyhedge Road, when Kelly reported that all was well. At about 3.30 am, the constable had completed the outward march of his beat and was walking away from the railway station. He later recalled that he saw a man a few yards away from the station, whose conduct awoke his suspicions. Kelly followed him along the road and attempted to arrest him. He later said, 'When I asked him what he was doing, the man hurried on.' The man ran away and, blowing his whistle to summon help, Kelly gave chase.

His quarry then hid himself among the trees which lined the road. The next Kelly knew of him was when he sprang out on his approach and drew an automatic. This was at the junction of Gunnersbury Lane and Pope's Lane. Three shots rang out and, at point blank range, they could not miss. Kelly fell to the ground, but not before he blew on his whistle again.

This incident must have taken place sufficiently near to the gates of Gunnersbury Park, because it was heard there and responded to by James Cleaver, who lived in Chiswick, and had been a private policeman-cum-watchman employed on the Rothschild estate for a few years. He was patrolling the grounds at night with Jim, his fox terrier. He heard the shots

Baron's Pond and Gunnersbury Avenue, Acton, 1920s. Paul Lang's collection

and the whistle and rushed to the source of these noises. He cannot have been far away, and was probably at the lodge gates, 220 yards from the scene of the shooting. On arrival, about two or three minutes later, he found Kelly's assailant still on the scene. He later recalled:

> I saw a man just a few paces away from me – running. His distance from me was six or seven paces. He was dressed as a soldier. … He looked to me more like an officer or a sergeant major, than a private. … It was too dark to see his face.

Cleaver struck at him with his knobbed stick, which was his only weapon, and though the man ducked, he received a blow on the back of the neck. The man then turned his gun on Cleaver and fired once more, hitting his mark and the bullet passed through his target's shoulder. Cleaver's dog jumped into the fray, but was kicked and then shot at, though the bullet missed this time.

The unknown man fled westwards along Pope's Lane. Cleaver had been unable to apprehend him, as he had a weak leg. He briefly went home to reassure his wife that all was well.

All this commotion attracted additional people. The railway night signalman, Mr Freeland and his colleague, a signal repair man, had been in the signal box that night and had initially thought the shots were the firing of a motor cycle engine. However, when they heard more shots, they changed their minds and went to see James Mitchell, the stationmaster, who lived in a house near to the railway station. Once the three had gathered together, a number of policemen had arrived at the station. They then went to the nightwatchman's hut.

Meanwhile, William Perryman, the nightwatchman, had been involved in the night's events already. He later recalled:

> I was on duty all night at the hut opposite Acton Town station. I came outside at 2.25 am and had a walk round. Everything was all right. At 3.28 I heard three shots and at 3.31 I heard three more, and within five or six minutes of the last lot of shots I saw a young man, clean shaven, about 30 respectably dressed, supporting a policeman who was staggering towards the hut with his head bent forward. The young man said 'This fellow has been shot.'

Apparently the two men then took Kelly into the hut, took off his coat and helmet and gave him a drink of water. Yet when the other policemen arrived, headed by a sergeant on a bicycle, the young man disappeared. It later transpired that this man was Mr F Hones of South Ealing, a bus clerk, on his way home from Kilburn. Kelly was asked who shot him and he replied, 'That bastard in the trench coat'. He was then taken, along with Cleaver, to Acton Cottage Hospital, which was further up Gunnersbury Lane, just south of Acton High Street. Cleaver was found by PC T Irvine, who had come from south Acton on hearing the shots. Cleaver told him, 'I'm shot, and there's one of your mates up the road who, I think, has also been shot.' It was at the cottage hospital there that the divisional surgeon, Dr W A Rudd, attended them. He decided that two of the wounds were dangerous.

Kelly had been hit in the stomach, the chest and the left leg, whilst Cleaver was wounded by a bullet which passed through his shoulder. Most of that morning was spent by Rudd

Acton Cottage Hospital, c.*1898.* Paul Lang's collection

operating on Kelly in order to remove the bullets and his condition was very serious indeed. Later that day he was sent to St Thomas's Hospital, being admitted at 5 pm. It was thought that he might need the transfusion of ten pints of blood, which ten of his fellow officers gladly provided, though it transpired this was not eventually necessary. The less badly hurt Cleaver was also seen to, but though suffering from loss of blood, he was not dangerously ill and so was sent home to recover, Rudd seeing him there.

The police combed the district for clues. The first discovery was that the office of the railway station had been broken into. The station had only one entrance from the main road. This was locked between one and four each morning and was barred by a pair of heavy steel expanding doors. However, the station had been broken into, with the steel doors' lock being forced, and the interior cloakroom door had been tampered with. The handle of the booking office safe had also been broken, though no money had been taken, and a suitcase in the left luggage section had been ransacked. A workman's suit was also found on the floor, though it had not necessarily been left by the burglar, who had probably only been on the premises for a few minutes. A Yale key had been used to try to open one of the doors, without success, and its broken remains were found there. The case, it transpired, had been deposited by two men on Monday, and they had not subsequently called for it. Ten mackintoshes had been taken and these were found in a brown canvas bag behind a recess near Gunnersbury House; probably dropped during the burglar's flight from the two men he shot. His spoils had been very minimal at best.

Shortly after the shootings, a flat in the nearby Denehurst Gardens was found to have been broken into. Jewellery from Mrs Lindop, wife of the occupant, had been taken. A man seen loitering nearby fitted the above description of the thief.

The police also found a screwdriver in the mud 600 yards west of Gunnersbury Lane, and a pair of pliers were located in a gully under a hedge. Whether these had any connection with the crime is another question. Spent cartridges were found at the scene of the shooting and one detective deduced that the bullets were made of nickel. A cap and a muffler were also found.

It is possible the guilty man was spotted later that morning. Robert Head, a conductor on the District line, reported that he was on a staff train at 4.20 am. Because he had heard of the robbery and shooting, he was on the alert. At Chiswick Park, the next station to the east, towards London, from Acton Town, he saw a man about 30 years old, five feet ten inches in height, and wearing a short khaki coat and a civilian cap. His boots were muddy. Head noticed him because he was not among the dozen or so regular passengers who were also there. He was sitting with his legs crossed, looking down and had no luggage. This stranger left at the next station, Hammersmith.

Another man also saw this suspect. He was a Mr Read, a Chiswick postman, who had arrived at Chiswick station at 4.20 and the gate was closed. When it was opened, Read was the first to enter. He was surprised to see a man already on the platform. He must have entered by climbing over the fence and up the embankment. Yet Read took little more notice of the man, and did not know of the robbery and shootings. He described the man thus: 'He was wearing a trench-coat – and, I think, an ordinary cap. He kept one hand in his coat pocket. I can say nothing of his age, height and general appearance.'

Whether this man was the same as the one 'with a big, sharp nose', who had been seen loitering near the station on Monday, as reported by local shopkeepers, was impossible to know. One Miss Campbell, a tobacconist's assistant, saw this man on the afternoon before the crime, staring hard at the booking office windows and loitering there for an hour. According to her, he was 24, wore a cap and a waterproof coat. Mr Bailey, a hairdresser, whose shop adjoined the station, also saw a man loitering nearby, and his description of the suspect matched that of Miss Campbell.

On the following day the police issued a description of the man they wanted, as given to them by the two injured policemen: 'Age about 25, height 5ft. 9in. or 10 in., clean shaven, slim build; dress trench coat and cap; smart appearance, may have injury at back of neck, and suffering from dog bites on leg.' Anyone who had such a man as a lodger, and who had been absent on Tuesday night or Wednesday morning, was encouraged to alert this to the police.

The police also thought that an ironmonger might be able to assist them in finding who had bought the wire cutters. They certainly seemed to have a number of individual characteristics. They were six inches long and half an inch wide. On the hinge part was stamped 'British make'. And '5/P' was marked on the outside part. These may have been the seller's private mark or a price mark. The screwdriver located had 'L' marked on its handle and also 'B and S., L'.

Kelly had the three bullets removed from his body on the Wednesday evening. He was stated to be doing well, though the wound in his abdomen seemed serious. He had been able to give his colleagues a brief description of his attacker and a short account of events on that morning, but did not think he would know him again. Sir Neil MacReady, the Commissioner, visited him in hospital and gave him the force's sympathy. His wife also visited him on the day of the shooting. Sir Charles Balance, a medical specialist, put him under his own direct charge, and was much troubled by Kelly's heavy vomiting. On 22 February, Kelly died in hospital and so the case became one of murder. His funeral service was held at

Westminster Cathedral. Author's collection

Westminster Cathedral, and the union and papal flags were at half mast on that occasion. About 1,000 of his colleagues, including MacReady, were present in what were 'impressive scenes'.

On Wednesday 24 March, the inquest was held at the Lambeth Coroner's Court. Dr Robinson of St Thomas's hospital explained that death was due to peritonitis, due to the bullet wounds, followed by gangrene. Evidence was given about the clues found and the description of the killer. The police had not been able to apprehend anyone for the crime, though enquiries were apparently continuing. The jury could only return a verdict of murder by person or persons unknown.

Clearly, the man responsible for this fatal shooting had not initially intended to kill. Yet he was prepared for the possibility that he might have to do so. He was a burglar, who was well equipped and had first stolen items from the suitcases from the railway station, though whether there was anything taken other than the mackintoshes is impossible to know. It seems that the theft of the mackintoshes was a fairly unimportant one; perhaps something else was there – or was thought to be there. Possibly the man sought something that the two men who had deposited there. He then left and walked up Gunnersbury Lane. Was he planning to commit another burglary? Probably. Seeing a policeman, his plans might have been thwarted, so he decided to act with maximum force. After he had had his encounter with the two men, it seems he then went on to steal jewellery from the house in Denehurst Gardens. At some point, he discarded the items taken from the station as being of little or no value to him, as well as his burglary tools. It was Kelly's ill luck that he came across the armed man on his beat. The killer may well have been the man who was seen at Chiswick station, on his return to the relative anonymity of London. The local press surmised that he was an experienced local thief.

CHAPTER 5

The IRA Murders, 1921

Let all spies and traitors beware.

Most people are aware of the IRA terrorist campaign in London in the 1970s and 1980s, which claimed the lives of 56 people and injured hundreds more. Yet there were Irish bombings in London in the Victorian era. More importantly for this book, there was the campaign which took place by the IRA in London in the early 1920s. Why was this? The IRA had been formed in January 1919 by Michael Collins (1890–1922) to fight the British for a free and united republic of Ireland. Much of this bitter conflict took place in Ireland. However, the IRA decided to bring the struggle to the heart of the British Empire and attacked civilians in London in 1921, an aspect of the struggle not acknowledged in recent high-profile films such as *Michael Collins* and *The Wind that Shakes the Barley*.

On the Sunday morning of 3 April 1921, George Tyrell, a young caddie, was walking along the golf links at Ashford. He was doubtless surprised to see a man lying down on the grass there. Calling to another caddie, Tyrell said, 'He's dead.' They called the police and in the mean time found four bullets on the road nearby which were later collected by the police. Dr Walker of Manor Road, Ashford, was quickly on the scene. He noted that the man had been dead for at least six hours. Dr Francis Thompson, the police surgeon, carried out the post mortem and noted the following wounds. There was a bullet wound on the right side of the body and two on the back. Thompson admitted that one of these could have been self-inflicted but the others could not have been. One bullet had been fired from within a few feet of the victim. There was also a white metal watch and chain, a white cigarette case and a diary, marked 'London and Lancashire Insurance Company', near the body. Initially the identity of the corpse was unknown. Arthur Howard, another caddie, found that near to the fourteenth bunker was a piece of paper which read 'Let all spies and traitors beware! – IRA'.

A woman identified only as Frances told the court who the victim was. She said, 'I identify the body as that of my cousin. He was 20 years of age and a clerk-book keeper.' She had last seen him alive on the evening of Saturday 2 April, between 6.30 and 6.45.

The inquest was held on 6 April, but after identification and cause of death had been given, it was adjourned until 20 April. The police wanted to know more about the victim and issued the following description of him in order to help jog someone's memory:

Age twenty one (looks older), height five feet eight or nine inches; complexion, pale; hair and slight moustache, dark brown; eyes grey; large prominent teeth, second tooth from the centre of the upper jaw missing, and the corresponding tooth on lower jaw. Dressed in blue serge suit; white soft collar, imitation gold safety pin therein, black tie with gold stripes, heliotrope shirt, yellow metal embossed sleeve links, brown mixture socks, black laced shoes, velvour hat, 'Dulcis' make inside.

It was learnt that the deceased, who went by the name of Stanton, among others, had attended an Irish dance at Kelvedon Hall, Kelvedon Road, Fulham, on the evening of Saturday 2 April. He was seen there at half past eight that evening, talking to two or three other men. Any further information was sorely needed.

The inquest was concluded on 20 April. It had since been learnt that the real name of the deceased was Vincent Fovarque. There were also grave security concerns about the inquest. Seven people involved in the inquiry, including jurymen, had been sent threatening letters. These letters declared that, if a certain verdict was reached, relatives of those people would be killed. The police took charge of the letters.

There were two principal witnesses at the inquest. One was Matthew Patrick Higgins, a young clerk, who had once served in the Irish Guards. From December 1920 until March 1921, he had been the secretary to the Irish Self Determination League, which was a body with links to the IRA. He revealed that Fovarque had introduced himself as Richard Stanton and had come to Kelvedon Hall in February 1921 for the Saturday dance there. Higgins had next seen him on 16 February at Fulham Town hall, during a meeting of the League. Finally, he recalled seeing him on the fatal evening of 2 April and recounted that, at about 8.15, Fovarque had been talking to some men in the outer lobby, but he did not know who they were, nor did he see them leave. He added that the deceased had lived in Chelsea and had not joined the League.

Michael McDonald, a clerk, introduced himself as the League's assistant secretary since January 1921. He said that the red ticket found on the deceased's body was a ticket given to him at the dance on 2 April. Fovarque was not seen dancing that evening, but he agreed that he had been seen in the hall. McDonald did not know him by the name of Stanton.

Detective Inspector Smith, who had been investigating the case, had failed to find any evidence against the killer/s and so

Kelvedon Road, 2008. Author's collection

the jury could only offer the verdict of 'Wilful murder against some person or persons unknown'.

It would seem that Fovarque was taken by the men he was last seen with to Ashford golf course late on the Saturday night, where no one could witness their shooting him. They believed that he had betrayed them, or was planning to do so. However, according to Higgins, Fovarque was not a member of the League. Presumably he was looking for secrets he could sell or pass on. With him having at least one alias, it would appear that he was living a shadowy and dangerous existence, as his ending proved. On another footing, perhaps his murder was the inspiration for Agatha Christie's second Poirot novel, *Murder on the Links*, in which a dead man, who has also been shot, is found on a golf course.

This was not the last of the IRA attacks in London. There was a wider campaign on the weekend of 14–15 May that year. Then there were attacks; both shooting individuals and burning property, in Catford, Shepherd's Bush, Blackheath, Tooting, Battersea and West Kensington. Some planning had gone into these attacks, for they were far from random. They were targeted at those who had relatives serving in Ireland.

At about a quarter to ten on Saturday 14 May, a gang of five masked men arrived at an address in Stowe Road, asking for a Mr Birthright, who had once been in the Royal Irish Constabulary. The man was not at home, but the men produced what was purported to be a warrant for his arrest, and then tried to set fire to the house with paraffin brought for that purpose. The flames were quickly extinguished and when calls for the police were made, the men ran away.

Their next port of call was to have deadlier results. Horace Macneil, aged 47, a railway engineer's foreman, lived with his wife in a house in Bloemfontein Road in Shepherd's Bush. His house was near to the Uxbridge Road, with its busy tram and omnibus routes. He was reasonably well off, and his will left £174 4s 10d to his widow. The pair were about to go to bed when there was a knock at the door. It was about 10 pm. Macneil answered it and saw four men on his doorstep. They were all fairly well dressed but, most sinisterly, wore masks or goggles to conceal their faces. He asked them what it was they

Bloemfontein Road, 2008. Author's collection

wanted. They told him they wished to see one Mr Cornes. This was Macneil's son-in-law, who had served in Ireland for a few months, and was currently in the motor transport section of the Royal Irish Constabulary. The householder explained that Cornes did not live there.

The men asked him where Cornes lived and, as the question was asked, two of the four edged into the house and into the hall. Macneil tried to close the front door but was unable to do so. Macneil later told the police:

> I went to the door and saw four men. I told them they had made a mistake, but one of them said, 'I am sure we have not made a mistake. I am going to shoot'. Another of them then said, 'Shoot low'. I cannot describe any of them.

Macneil gave another version of his statement:

> Someone said 'Is – here?' My wife said, 'You have made a mistake. Go round to – (another address)'. I tried to push them out of the door and one said, 'I'll shoot'. The other man said 'No' and one man said, 'Shoot low'. I saw four

men altogether. The one that fired was about 30 and 5 foot 8 inches. I think he was clean shaven, dark, dark clothes and a soft felt hat. I thought it was a drunken affair, nothing like this.

Macneil fell backwards once shot and was caught in his wife's arms. The gang's leader was referred to as 'captain'. He and his men all seemed to be Irish, judging by their accents.

What was indisputable was that Macneil was shot in the abdomen. The four intruders then ran in the direction of the Uxbridge Road. They left behind them two revolvers and two bottles of petrol. At least one neighbour saw the gang members, but could not describe them, except to say that they wore dark clothing and were all young men. Mrs Macneil then went to her husband's help. The wounded man was taken to the West London Hospital. He was operated on at once for perforation of the bowels. After the bullet had been located, there were hopes he would recover. However, he died on the morning of Wednesday 18 May of bronchial pneumonia, following the injury.

After the attack at the Macneils, the gang visited an address in Fairholme Road, West Kensington. As before, they asked for the householder, one Captain Wood, who was absent, serving in Ireland. They pushed their way into the house and searched it. Before leaving they tried to set it on fire, but with little effect. The men's leader had an Irish accent.

Enquiries into his murder began three days later, but were hampered by the lack of information because people were frightened to come forward. It was noted, 'it is very difficult to get evidence. People seem to be terrorised, and are afraid of assassins entering their homes and shooting them. It is quite a natural fear.' At the inquest, which began at Hammersmith on 21 May, the coroner urged the press to use the utmost discretion in printing details of names and addresses of witnesses. Other precautions were taken. Police guarded the entrance to the court and none were allowed inside without a permit.

Mrs Macneil was the principal witness and she said that her husband had no connection with Irish politics, nor had he written any letters to anyone in Ireland. She had written to her son-in-law there. She knew of no one who had a grudge against her husband, who was not a quarrelsome man. She recollected that two of the intruders were aged 20–23, respectably dressed, with dark blue suits and black velvour hats. They wore big goggles and smeared glasses, so she could not see any of their faces. One was fair haired and had a long face. Each man had a revolver, with the barrels protruding from their pockets, and carried brown paper parcels.

Another witness recalled hearing a sound like an explosion and then seeing three men leaving the house. They were running too quickly for him to be able to recognize them. Two of the men had brown parcels in their left hands, but nothing in their right hands. Macneil's earlier statements were read out in court. The gang split up; some ran down Rainsbury Road and others Ellerslie Road. They may have fled to a waiting motor car, though in their flight they left behind an American Colt revolver and an army issue revolver. There were five cartridges in one and four in another, so presumably a total of three bullets were fired in the brief encounter. It was thought that the latter gun fired the fatal shot. These two guns were handed in by an unknown person.

There was much sympathy for the Macneils, as shown at the funeral on 23 May. The cortege began at the family home, held by two mounted policemen, followed by Macneil's colleagues, totalling some hundreds of railway workers, then there were three carriages for the family. Hundreds of onlookers manned the funeral route. Many wreaths from different people and organizations were placed on the grave. Macneil had been well known in the locality for many years, having served his engineering apprenticeship at Thorneycroft's Works in Chiswick. His life had been cruelly cut short through no fault of his own.

And that was that. Nothing more was discovered of these crimes and the perpetrators were never brought to justice. It was noted in the following year, in a review of London crimes of 1921, 'It will be seen that the only two unsolved cases in the metropolitan area were political in origin, and there is no class of crime more difficult to track down, because there is no strong line leading to any one individual.' The police did take action, raiding the headquarters of the Irish Self Determination League in Shaftesbury Avenue, finding papers there, some written in Erse and some in code. Twelve men and four women were arrested in London. It was believed that the gunmen were from Ireland and that they were helped in London by female sympathizers. There were a number of well organized and well funded Sinn Fein organizations in the capital and their aim was to threaten relatives of members of the armed forces, to whom the police offered protection. This type of crime did claim another victim, a high-profile one, too, when General Sir Henry Wilson was shot dead in front of his London home in June 1921. His attackers were apprehended and nearly lynched. With the emergence of the Irish Free State later that year, these crimes came to an end, having achieved little of merit.

CHAPTER 6

Murder in Shoreditch? 1923

She was a good woman and did not deserve it.

In August 1923, Edith Emms, a 37-year-old waitress, was facing a life-changing dilemma. She wondered whether she should return to her estranged husband. She explained this to Thomas Allan, a regular at Gillman's cafe on Lamb Conduit Street, in which she worked. 'I have heard from my husband Jack, he's coming home. I don't know what I am going to do, whether to go back with him or not.'

Although the couple had a son, John, aged 17 who was an invalid, resident in Folkestone, she was not necessarily better off living with her husband. John Emms was born in about 1882 and his stated occupation was as a driver. They had married in 1905 and separated seven years later. Shortly afterwards, he went to Australia in order to better himself. Yet he fell into crime there and was sent to prison in Melbourne for burglary in 1914. Four years later he was in jail again, this time for four years, for theft and for receiving stolen goods. He was released in 1922 and returned to his mother's house in Bethnal Green in the summer of the following year. When he was in Australia, he had corresponded with his wife, but they had ceased to communicate with each other in 1920.

Yet he now seemed a more attractive proposition. He had at least £400 with him, very possibly made by illegal means. Furthermore, he knew how to turn on the charm when he had to. He appeared to Edith to be a different man and he promised to treat her differently. They would buy a business together and start anew. Edith was also given a neck chain and jewellery. The two began to live together; perhaps a fatal decision.

They opened a small restaurant/coffee house at Hackney Road in Shoreditch on 28 September 1923, having paid £250

Hackney Road, 2008. Author's collection

for it. Elizabeth Hitch, a 28-year-old kitchen maid, was employed at £1 per week. They also had two paying lodgers, both single men. These were Arthur Casseltine, a 27-year-old music hall attendant at the Poplar Hippodrome, and Arthur Fowler, a 30-year-old tailor's assistant who worked in Hackney Road. Between them, they paid 35s a week in rent.

Relations between the recently reunited husband and wife were poor. Elizabeth recalled, 'I have seen Mr Emms slap Mrs Emms on her face in his temper.' On another occasion, when her mistress had a black eye, Edith explained:

> Jack done it, you don't know what I have to put up with. I was sitting in the armchair last night, he smacked my face, and then threw the record at me, which hit me in the face, he burnt my fur, and he made me pawn all my jewellery. I am sorry I ever came back to live with him.

She was certainly frightened, and said that if there was no one else in the house:

> I shall be left alone with him by myself, and I am dead frightened of him, he often frightens me, if I am asleep when

he comes home at night, he creeps upstairs and stands in the room with his big brown eyes, staring at me, also puts his hands at the side of his head. Don't be surprised Lylie, if you come home one morning and find me dead, I am so frightened of him.

Additionally, on 20 November, Allan stated that Edith had a black eye and 'appeared in great distress'. Finally, Elizabeth Mockett was told by her, 'That's where he hit me. He is always knocking me about.'

The fact that the business was running into problems made matters worse. They were falling behind in the payment of rates and taxes, and Elizabeth had to be fired from her job. Edith wrote to her friend Allan (who stated, 'There has never been any immorality between Edith and myself, neither has there been any suggestion of same'). The postcard read, 'Dear Mr Allan, Could you meet me Saturday night at 8 o'clock the corner of Red Lion Street, Holborn end'. It is not certain if they met nor what the outcome was, if they did. However, on 18 November the business was sold, at a loss, for £200, to one Mr Dodd.

Matters came to a head on 22 November. Casseltine had left at 9.15 am and was on duty at the music hall, 5.20–11.20 pm. Fowler left the house five minutes earlier than Casseltine and was at work until 1 pm, when he returned to his lodgings for something to eat. From 6 to 11.15 pm he was out at the Vaudeville Theatre. Both did not return home until almost midnight. They were making their supper when their landlord appeared and made a joke about them using so much milk in their drinks that it was no wonder the business had not done well.

Minutes later, at about midnight, Emms went up to the bedroom and found his wife lying on the floor of the bedroom, dead. He later explained, 'I saw my wife lying on the floor with her feet partly under the bed, with only her chemise and night dress on. I endeavoured to arouse her but failed, so I shouted downstairs to the lodgers to go for a policeman.' When the police arrived, Mr Emms told them that there had been a burglary and his wife had probably died from the fright.

Certainly this was not impossible, for the large room in which she was found was in a state of disarray – clothes were strewn in the floor, the cupboards had been ransacked and a chair was overturned – and the gate at the back of the premises had been smashed in. Apparently, 'The shop and side door showed no signs of forceable entry, but a door, leading from Barnes Road at a yard at the rear of the premises, showed signs of being forced.' Money was apparently missing, though a few copper coins were found on the floor. Emms said that there was a cup in the fireplace which usually had £5 in it, the cash box in the wardrobe was empty and there was no money in his wife's apron for the shop's takings, which were usually about £2 per day.

Dr Robert Bronte carried out the post mortem. At first he would not commit himself to stating the cause of death. Privately, he stated 'death may have been caused by shock or a fright, or by a blow on the abdomen, which might cause the heart to cease beating'. The contents of the stomach were sent to the government analyst for further investigation.

The inquest began on 27 November at Bethnal Green by Dr Edwin Smith, coroner for North East London. Matilda Hatch of Warwick Road, Forest Gate, and mother of the deceased, gave formal evidence of identification. She had last seen her daughter on 14 November and said that she seemed well, but had complained that she was 'going mad with worry'. With that, the inquest was adjourned until 8 December.

Then, Mrs Hatch elaborated on the nature of her daughter's worries, which concerned the business and the possibility that she might split up from her husband. They had quarrelled, her husband had thrown a bad egg at her face, and there was a bruise on her face. Yet Mrs Hatch had to state that she had never heard Emms threaten her daughter. Even so, Emms had taken the precaution of having a solicitor present.

Edith's movements on the fatal evening were recounted. Mary Emms, her husband's mother, called at 5.30 pm and thought her daughter-in-law was depressed over business matters and was prey to other fears. Apparently Edith said, 'I often feel I could take a dose and get myself out of it'. William Learner and his wife spent the rest of the evening with Edith, only leaving her at a quarter to eleven. They thought Edith was 'apparently in her usual health', a rather ambiguous remark. Yet Elizabeth Learner reported that she remarked, 'If I had the pluck I would put my head in the gas oven.' They left at either 10.25 or 10.45, accounts varying.

Medical matters then surfaced. Dr J O'Dwyer stated that a microscopic examination showed that there was no evidence of physical violence on the body. It was true that she was not in perfect health, and there was fatty degeneration of the heart muscles. These could lead to early death. However, he could not discover the cause of death. It might have been fright or shock. If she had received a blow to the abdomen, death might have resulted if the heart had stopped beating. John Webster, the government analyst from the Home Office, said that he had analysed the stomach content and had found no evidence of poison. The police report said that 'There were no marks on the body and he [Dr O'Dwyer] was of the opinion that there was no sign of foul play.'

Evidence was gathered from two other witnesses. Fowler recalled seeing the corpse in the room on the night of the murder and recalled, 'She was a good woman and did not deserve it.' When questioned as to what he meant by this remark, he explained that he thought that her sudden death had been caused by burglars who had broken in. A different interpretation was suggested by Elizabeth Hitch, who had been once employed as a housemaid by the Emms. She said that she had seen Mrs Emms being hit twice by her husband and that she was in fear of him.

Emms then gave his version of events on the fateful day. He had been absent from home that evening, only returning at midnight. Unpleasant as he was, it seems unlikely that he had the opportunity to murder his wife, as his movements were accounted for by others.

At 3.50 pm he had left home and went to Covent Garden and Piccadilly. It was here that he met Peggy Lee, a prostitute, and they went back to her flat on Baker Street. She alleged he stole from her and would not pay her 'for the use of her body', though Emms claimed that she stole from him. Before he left, he asked Flossie Athos, Peggy's maid, for sex, offering two

Baker Street, 2008. Author's collection

shillings, but she refused. At 7.30 pm, he was in the Crown and Anchor, Bethnal Green. Fifteen minutes later, he visited his brother William and the two went back to the pub, where they spent the rest of the evening. They then went to an eel shop on Bethnal Green Road, and Emms returned home just before midnight. En route, he met a policeman, PC James Cornwell, on Virginia Road, and asked for directions (presumably he was a little drunk).

He recounted how he found his wife, and believing she was dead, asked his lodgers to call the police. He said that he and his wife had been on good terms, though 'they had a few words occasionally'. These were over cooking. Both of them liked drinking. He denied ever hitting her, but confessed, oddly enough, to having thrown gramophone records at her.

If this was a case of burglary, then the thieves would have had to have known the house well enough to have been able to have purloined the cash. The jury at the inquest thought that this might have been so. Yet Elizabeth Madolski and Israel Tendler, the Emms's neighbours, saw nothing on the fatal night and heard nothing unusual.

Detective Inspector Smith wrote that 'The coroner then suggested to the jury that they should return an open verdict, as the evidence failed to disclose the cause of death and this course they finally adopted.' Privately, he wrote, 'The enquiry is being continued, and should anything further transpire, a report will at once be submitted.'

Edith was a woman of admittedly nervous temperament. She may have been frightened to death by burglars, or by another cause. It seems almost impossible that her unpleasant husband was responsible, unless we can imagine he could have returned home and in a few minutes have caused his wife's death, knowing full well that the two lodgers were on the premises. Burglars seem a more likely explanation, but as to who they were, it is impossible to know. However, the neighbours heard nothing suspicious, so even the existence of the burglars must remain questionable.

CHAPTER 7

An Acrobat's Death, 1924

he was inclined to quarrel and fight when intoxicated

I n a tourist guide to London of 1927, it was stated that, 'Leicester Square and Soho have long been famous as the home of a colony of French, Italians and Swiss. Hereabouts are many excellent restaurants frequented not only by foreigners but by Londoners themselves.' Soho was also the scene of several crimes featured in this book.

At half past eleven on Friday night, 27 June 1924, PC Thurston was in Sherwood Street and was told of a man lying in a pool of blood nearby. He found the fatally wounded Martial Lechevalier, a 26-year-old French acrobat, on Air Street, near Piccadilly Circus. He died shortly afterwards, before he reached Charing Cross Hospital. Just after the

Air Street, 2008. Author's collection

stabbing, one Mary Allen saw the dying man and heard him speaking to another man in French, a language she did not understand. Genazzini Flavio, an Italian waiter on his way home after work, said that he, too, saw the body and when Lechevalier was asked by another who was responsible, he merely answered, 'I don't know. I don't know' in poor English.

According to his brother, Paul Edward Lechevalier, a tailor of Grafton Street, he had come to England in March of that year, before briefly returning to France and then was in England from early June. He had allegedly supported himself with funds he had with him, and money given to him by his two brothers, one of whom was in France. He was not known to have been in employment. However, Paul had seen little of his brother, did not even know his address and said, 'My brother was always very reticent and did not say very much about his affairs.' He had not seen him since 2 June, when he had seen him outside the Palace Theatre on Cambridge Circus.

Chief Inspector Frederick Wensley of Scotland Yard and Chief Inspector Brown were in charge of the case and they

Piccadilly Circus, 1920s. Paul Lang's collection

requested that Samuel Ingleby Oddie (1869–1945), the Westminster coroner, adjourn the inquest which had opened on 1 July, for two weeks. After the official identification of the body, their wish was granted.

On the following day, the police issued a statement that they wanted to talk to one Alfred Sauvaget, a 29-year-old Frenchman. He was five feet nine inches tall, of stout build, clean shaven, with dark hair and was last seen in a grey suit and a trilby hat. Apparently he had been seen with Lechevalier on the evening of his death. In the early hours of 28 June, he and another man had gone to an address in Gerrard Street in a taxi. He had also been seen at an address in St Martin's Lane on 30 June, but was said to have been usually found in Torrington Square.

The adjourned inquest concentrated on the medical details of the case. Dr Henry Weir submitted his report of the post mortem. There was a wound in the right side of the neck. It was four inches deep. Part of the bone was exposed. Death had resulted from a haemorrhage from this wound. A sharp weapon, such as a razor or knife, must have been used by his attacker. Given that Lechevalier was right-handed, the injury could not have been self-inflicted. The blow had been delivered from behind the victim, probably by a man who was right-handed. It was alleged that the crime had been witnessed by a woman who lived near Manchester and she was urged to tell the police what she knew.

More information was found out about the victim. Lechevalier had been born on 3 October 1897 at Asnieres, and later resided in Lille. He had a criminal record in France, for four charges. He had deserted from the army in 1918 twice, though was pardoned at the Armistice. Then he was charged with living off prostitutes' earnings in the same year and finally with brawling in 1922. He was fined and spent time in prison for the last offence.

He was registered in London as an alien, i.e. a foreigner. He claimed he had come to England 'to study the English language'. Although registered as living at Castle Street, he actually lived with a Mrs Burns, aged 24, at Albany Street (the two had first met in 1922). Mrs Burns had been born Helene

Albany Street, 2008. Author's collection

Charheure in France and was a prostitute. She had arrived in England on 2 October 1923 and went through an arranged marriage with a John Burns on 2 April 1924, in order to become a British subject. When questioned, the woman claimed she had no knowledge of Lechevalier, but eventually confessed she had lived with him. As was said, 'Mrs Burns, as she then became, continued her immoral life and there is no doubt that she helped to support Martial Lechevalier'.

It would seem that Lechevalier was a criminal who was involved in the vice trade. Certainly, his associates, Sauvaget and Raymond Mathieu, a 29-year-old 'salesman' of Grafton Street, were arrangers of marriages between foreign prostitutes and British men. This arrangement was necessitated by the Aliens Act of 1905 which allowed undesirable foreigners to be deported. Foreign prostitutes who married British men could not be deported, and the women became indebted to the gang members who then made money out of them. Frank Keller was also associated with the gang and said, 'This gang numbers about 20. They are all desperate men. They are better known in France and the majority have been convicted there.'

Grafton Street, 2008. Author's collection

Another month was to pass before further evidence was presented to the coroner. This was because the police needed time to find crucial witnesses. Various accounts of Lechevalier's last hours were eventually recounted by a number of men. It was Mrs Burns who told of his activity during the daytime. At 2 pm he had left her lodgings to go to the cinema. He returned at 7.30 pm, having been elsewhere, as he was clearly the worse for wear and was very excited. She 'asked him not to go out any more as I knew that he was inclined to quarrel and fight when he was intoxicated'. But he refused to heed her and left their rooms shortly afterwards, at about 7.45 pm.

Auguste Guilleaume Pascall, a Frenchman who had lived in England for 24 years, who described himself as a hotel keeper of the New North Road, Theobald's Road, was the first to give his story. He said that he was with Lechevalier on the fatal night. They had met at Belmont's pub on Dean Street at half past eight. Mathieu was the first there, and then Lechevalier. Another man known as Fredo later appeared. Pascall had been acquainted with him for seven months. They spent the evening talking and drinking, in at least four other pubs. The last to be

The Palace Theatre, 2008. Author's collection

visited was the Cock on Shaftesbury Avenue, which they left at about ten to eleven. Earlier, he claimed that Lechevalier talked about a man who he meant to fight later that night, but Pascall told him not to be silly, for if he did the police would be after him. Pascall then went home to an address in St Martin's Lane. He claimed that none of them were drunk.

Although he went to bed, he was awoken at two by Fredo, who asked for Mathieu's address. Pascall told him that the man lived in Grafton Street (where Lechevalier's brother also resided), but asked why he needed to know that information at such an hour. Fredo said that there had been a fight.

Mathieu was the next to speak, and he spoke little English, so an interpreter had to be used. He recalled meeting Lechevalier at a pub on Old Compton Street. Fredo and Pascall were with him, as well as two other Frenchmen. When the group split up, Mathieu, Lechevalier and a man known only as 'the little fellow' went up Shaftesbury Avenue. When they reached Rupert Street, 'the little fellow', who was walking behind Lechevalier, said, 'He has got on my nerves with his language'. He then hit Lechevalier across the mouth and drew blood. Mathieu calmed them down and suggested they had a drink. Reaching Little Pulteney Street, Mathieu left them for a time and when he returned he saw a shocking sight.

The 'little fellow' raised his hand, which held a knife or razor, and drew it swiftly across Lechevalier's neck. He then swiftly ran off. Lechevalier pulled his handkerchief across his neck and told Mathieu, 'Raymond, take me to hospital'. He then collapsed to the ground and said 'I want to sleep'. He said no more. Mathieu remained with him until the police arrived and he gave them his name and address. He then went home and in the early hours was awoken by Fredo, who wanted to know exactly how much the 'little one' knew. Apparently this unknown man had told Fredo 'Lechevalier had struck me on the nose and I gave him a good cut'. Fredo apologised on the man's behalf that he had left Mathieu with the body. Mathieu was asked to describe the 'little one'. He said that he was fat, with a round face and a broken nose. His complexion was yellow and he was wearing a brown suit and a soft hat.

Mrs Marie Pugh of William Street told the jury that she did charring for a French woman, Mrs Yvonne Harper, a prostitute of Shaftesbury Avenue. Mrs Pugh knew that Fredo was a frequent visitor to Mrs Harper's abode. She recollected that on the 29 and 30 June, the two had been together in Whitfield Street and that Fredo had had blood on his clothes. Mrs Harper explained that Fredo had sent her a note telling her to meet him there. Apparently Mrs Harper had married one Edwin Harper in January 1923, but denied she had paid him to do so in order to remain in the country. She had not seen her husband for some time and did not know his current whereabouts.

The police wanted to talk to Fredo, and this they were unable to do until after this third sitting of the inquest had been adjourned. Fredo, whose real name was Albert Sauvaget, mentioned above, appeared at the final hearing of the inquest on 18 September, bringing a solicitor with him. He had been previously interviewed at Vine Street police station on 29 August and had signed a statement in the presence of Detective Inspector Charles Tanner. On 27 June, Sauvaget recalled being with a group of men including a fruit merchant called Frankau and an estate agent by the name of Streuser, and one Alexander. They had met Lechevalier, Pascall and Mathieu and two other men not known to him.

They had several drinks in a variety of pubs, before parting. He recalled having last seen Lechevalier at about a quarter to eleven in the Cock on Shaftesbury Avenue. He thought that previously Lechevalier had seemed nervous and had been drinking heavily. He claimed not to know about the assault until about half an hour after midnight when, on leaving a cafe, a man came up to him and made a gesture like the cutting of a throat and said 'Your friend'. He then took a taxi to see Pascall in order to find out what had happened.

Sauvaget said that he had known Lechevalier for ten years and had not quarrelled with him on the night of the murder. He explained that the reason why he had not come forward earlier was because he had been in France about the revision of his pension for a war wound. As soon as he knew the police wanted to see him, he returned to London, or so he said.

Oddie was unsatisfied with the evidence given by Pascall, Mathieu, Mrs Harper and Sauvaget, believing much of it to be a tissue of lies. The police agreed, 'owing to the bad character of the available witnesses they were most reticent'. The killer, if we believe Mathieu, was the anonymous fat man called 'the little one'. Whether it was or not, he was never traced. Why Lechevalier was killed was another matter and it may have been because the killer became annoyed with his would-be victim on the night of his death and the fight followed a quarrel between the two men. Or it could have been prearranged, as Lechevalier had mentioned having to fight someone later that evening. He seems to have been disposed to do so, with not only Mrs Burns remarking upon it, but also his brother, saying that he was 'very exciteable and quarrelsome' when drunk. Yet no one would come forward, despite the fact that 'it seems to be common knowledge among certain members of the French colony in Soho who the actual culprit is'. Yet, 'there is none upon which any charge can be made against any person now in this country'.

One suspect was an Algerian, aged between 27 and 30, five feet eight inches in height, with a pale complexion, dark hair and with a scar on his chin. He was well dressed and had apparently threatened Lechevalier, saying 'I have got it in for you'. One Fred Clarke claimed he had seen this man with Lechevalier on the night of the murder.

As a footnote to this case, in October 1925, one Giovanni Pergilore, a 37-year-old acrobat was accused of witnessing the stabbing. Pergilore was himself a criminal, being involved in a gang which extorted money from cafe owners. An accomplice of his was Wilfred Cooper, a 28-year-old waiter. Both were allegedly involved with the Sabini gang. Nothing came from this lead, however.

Finally, one D Lester of Duke Street apparently wrote to the police in 1928, telling them that the killer was still at large and associated with prostitutes at Jermyn Street. Yet on investigation it was found that there was no such man as D Lester. PS John Sands wrote, 'The murder of Martial Lechevalier was thoroughly investigated at the time and has been the subject of numerous enquiries since but no information has come into our possession upon which a charge could be substantiated against any person.' There was another anonymous letter found by one Victor Gillett, stating, 'The murderer of the Frenchman in Glasshouse street is a tall dark haired man in a white smock in a fish shop at the top of Beak Street. He is an Italian. THE MURDERER. VRG'. As with the other information sent to the police following the murder, it proved of no use.

CHAPTER 8

The Death of a Landlady, 1924

I feel strongly that this man should be under observation.

To the north of Euston railway station is a little square called Harrington Square. Since the 1890s, at least, one house on that square had been held as leasehold property by a Mrs Grace Goodall. It was in rather poor repair. In 1924, she was aged 73 and had been living apart from her husband, John Edward Goodall (said to be an artist and living in Berkhamstead, aged 71) for some years. Indeed, the two had not met since 1917. He rarely came up to London. She made money by renting out the eight rooms in her house. To do this, she advertised vacancies in the *YMCA Journal*, doubtless to attract a moral type of young man. She also owned three cottages in Chipping, near Buntingford, had £54 in savings and £20 in ready cash. According to PC Thurley, she was eccentric and often complained to the police about children and dogs causing a nuisance near her home.

We now turn to her lodgers. One was James Charles Kellaway, an elderly piano tuner who was only occasionally in employment. He had lived at Mrs Goodall's for about 25 years. Just before Mrs Goodall went to the Middlesex Hospital in 1912 for a serious operation, she made her will and the principal beneficiary was Kellaway. Another lodger was Louis John Midgley, a chef at the Hotel Russell. Another was Minno Lally, an Indian. In early December 1924, Mrs Goodall and Lally had quarrelled, when she had found that he was betting. This resulted in him finding new lodgings. However, he returned on 18 December to retrieve a photograph he had left behind.

Mrs Goodall had made an appointment at noon on Tuesday 23 December with one George Edwin Adams, a young electrical engineer of Hampstead Road, in order to discuss the

Harrington Square, 2008. Author's collection

installation of electricity in the house; apparently on 27 October she had contracted with him to have the work done. He arrived and broached the topic with Mrs Goodall in the house's lobby. To his surprise, he found that she no longer required his services for the London house, but might have some electrical work in one of her country properties. Adams told her that she might still have to pay for the work that she had agreed to have done, even if it were not. The two argued, and Adams later recalled, 'She got out of temper with me and I think I did with her.' After about five or six minutes (although on one occasion, he declared the meeting took twenty minutes), Adams said that he left the house and then went to the Horse Shoe pub on New Oxford Street.

Kellaway was in the house just after noon, and he was passing through the hall when he heard a conversation between Mrs Goodall and a young man, 20–23 years old, about five feet four inches in height and dressed in black. Kellaway recalled that Mrs Goodall had said that she had made an appointment to see two young men about current vacancies and doubtless he thought that this man was a prospective tenant. He, too, left the house, at about 12.30 and went to King Street Baths, leaving there at 2. He then had lunch with a Mr Lacey, finishing at about 3 pm.

Midgley, having finished his shift at the hotel, returned to his lodgings. He arrived at about 3 pm and was in the hallway, sorting through a pile of letters on the table. He then heard groans and went to their source, in the basement, by the kitchen door. It was there that he found his landlady. She was unconscious and huddled up, her face covered with blood. He then left the house to telephone for an ambulance and returned 20 minutes later.

Kellaway arrived at the house between 3.30 and 4 pm. He said to his landlady, 'What's the matter, Mrs Goodall?' The only other occupant of the house that afternoon had been Patrick McDonall, a travelling postal worker, and he had been asleep in the daytime so had heard nothing. None of the other tenants, mostly clerks, were in the house until the evening. Mrs Goodall had her wounds dressed by the ambulance men and was then taken to the London Temperance Hospital, being admitted at 4 pm. She had sustained serious injuries to the head, with a fractured skull.

At the scene of the crime, there was blood on the stairs and at the top of the landing was a shoe, a woollen cap which Mrs Goodall usually wore in the house, and three hair combs.

The hospital staff asked her how she had been injured. She said, 'A stranger came about a room. I proceeded him downstairs, when he struck me three times on the head.' Yet she admitted to Sister Ellie Bowers, 'I think I fell downstairs'. She also talked about a quarrel with a lodger, who was a stranger to her, and used the word 'bash' several times. How much weight should be put upon these words? She was described as being in a dazed and confused condition at the time of these utterances. When pressed for more details, she said, 'Go away, I want some sleep.'

Mrs Goodall died in hospital on 25 December. Dr John Pinkerton said that the cause of death was laceration of the brain, caused by severe wounds to the top and back of the head. These may have been caused by a fall on two separate occasions, but the injury to the top of the head might have been the result of a blow by a blunt instrument. One witness said that the deceased was subject to giddy fits and so might have fallen down the stairs.

The police thought that the man or men who were interested in the vacant rooms might have useful information. They appealed for them or anyone who knew of them, to come forward so that their identity could be established. Anyone who had seen a person leaving the house between 12.30 and 3pm should also come forward. Superintendent Hammett of Albany Street Police Station was named as being the principal point of contact. Yet the theory of prospective lodgers was queried by Hanna Granger, a servant, who had seen Mrs Goodall on the morning of the tragedy. According to her, the old lady had not spoken to her of any such new tenants, and that was something she would normally have mentioned.

The inquest began on Saturday afternoon of 27 December, at St Pancras Coroner's Court before Sir Walter Schroder. John William Kemperton, a builder and decorator of Paddington, made the formal identification of his deceased sister. He added that he thought she had some jewellery, but no silver plate, and that she lived alone, save for the lodgers. Midgley told how he found the body and Kellaway told what he knew, suggesting Mrs Goodall had an appointment with prospective tenants on that day. The inquest was then adjourned.

One possible clue was a pair of rubber gloves, which were found at the scene of the crime. Kellaway said he had never seen them before. However, there was a divergence of views as to whether these gloves were ones worn by ladies or by electricians. When questioned, Adams denied that he had rubber gloves. Two lodgers stated that they had seen Mrs Goodall wear them when doing the housework.

A number of witnesses came forward. One was Cecil Wiltshire, a milkman, who remembered seeing, at about a quarter to one, a tall man of medium build wearing a blue overcoat and a grey cap leaving the house. This may have been Adams. George Martin of Hampstead Road told the police that a 30-year-old man, five feet five inches in height and with an American accent, had called at his house on 10 December, asking for Mrs Goodall's address.

Although Adams contacted the police on 29 December about his visit to the house on the day of the murder, he seems to have become the leading suspect. He was newly married and had one child. His workshop at Litchfield Road was searched and a hammer, with red stains on it, was found there. However, on examination, these were found not to be blood. His clothes and other instruments were also investigated, but again, nothing incriminating could be found.

Hampstead Road, 2008. Author's collection

Adams was an epileptic. He had first had a fit in 1918 and had been treated at St George's Hospital. Views on Adams varied. One Charles Courtney, a caterer, stated that Adams was 'a very highly strung young man and very exciteable' and 'quick tempered'. Nellie Pickford had heard Adams threaten to kill his father, who had once been in prison, and that his father was concerned about his son. However, Effie Whyman, though agreeing that he was quick tempered and argumentative, said he was not violent. After an examination, Dr Maughan pronounced:

This man is mentally backward and mentally unstable.... He gets depressed and cries at times. He wants to wrestle after a 'fit' and may act violently if drunk or annoyed. Consciousness is partially suspended at times, though he goes on with his walk or work ... I feel strongly that this man should be under observation. There was nothing in my examination of the man last night that would justify me in ruling out the possibility, the probability of the man having used violence towards the woman.

Kellaway suspected the Indian ex-lodger, as he had a grudge against Mrs Goodall. Yet he spent the day of the crime with two Indian doctors, who were prepared to give him an alibi. It also seems rather extreme to commit murder over the fact that she ejected him from his lodgings and was not eager to return his photograph that he had left behind.

The police also received a curious letter about the murder, which was postmarked Wandsworth at 3.15 pm on 9 January 1925. It read:

Sir – I confess to the murder of Mrs Grace Goodall, on December 23. This has preyed on my mind since that awful day. Mr Churn who was with me threatens to murder me so I am resolved to end it all. Good Luck to the Police.
    Stanley Williams.

The police were unable to follow up this clue, if indeed it was a clue and not the work of hoaxers, who are all too common following an unsolved murder.

Oddly enough, there is no reference to Mrs Goodall's husband being questioned, if only as a matter of routine. Surely he must have been, but there is no surviving record of this.

The inquest was concluded after four sessions, the final one being on 1 February. The verdict was that this was a case of murder by person or persons unknown. It was never solved, but there seem to be three distinct possibilities as to who might have been responsible. First, Adams might have been guilty. He was the last man who was definitely known to have seen Mrs Goodall alive. He was known to be argumentative and violent. He had had an argument with her and was certainly disappointed about not being given the work that he believed she had promised him. As against that, he did contact the police without having had to, and there was no direct evidence against him, in the form of forensic evidence or witnesses. Secondly, could Kellaway have been responsible? He certainly had a strong motive, as he stood to inherit Mrs Goodall's property (and did indeed do so), worth £635 17s 11d. He also was in the house about the time of the murder and could have attacked Mrs Goodall after Adams left. Yet the same objections apply; there was nothing directly against him. Finally, if we take the victim's own testimony as being accurate, then the killer was the man who came in answer to the advert about a room being let. Quite why he killed her is a mystery, however, and there is no obvious motive for such a random attack. Theft does not seem to have been the reason for her death. Perhaps he was mentally unbalanced. Of the three possibilities, this seems the least improbable, but it does not lead us to the identity of the guilty party.

CHAPTER 9

The Poisoned Egg Merchant, 1926

He simply behaved like a madman all the time

Kusel Behr had been born in Lithuania in about 1878. In 1909 he married one Minda, aged 33, in Latzkov, Lithuania. They travelled around the world for a few years; to America, South Africa and Shanghai, before settling in London in 1916. Here, they acquired a permanent address at Lyndale Hall, 'a very large residence' on Finchley Road, Hampstead. He made his money in a partnership with Samuel (1871–1942), his elder brother, importing eggs from Europe and China to sell in Britain, presumably on a very large scale. From 1916 to 1920, they had been partners with the Matthew family, but the latter were bought out in 1920. In pursuit of this business, the two brothers often travelled widely and the business had branches in Berlin, Paris, Hamburg and Shanghai. Behr and Minda had four children; two boys, aged 15 and 16, a daughter living with them, Ethel aged 13, and a younger girl aged 9. They had at least three servants; Annie Gaffney, a parlour maid who had been in their employ since February 1925, Hannah Russ, a cook, and one Anna Zabrodoff, a Russian governess, who looked after their children, and had done so since 1918, after she fled from the Bolsheviks. Behr had a high opinion of Zabrodoff. The Behrs were well off, for they could also afford to employ nurses when required and had a telephone at home. Unlike most people in this book, this was an affluent middle-class family and at death Behr left over £20,000.

Yet, just the same, tragedy was to strike the family. Behr returned home one afternoon; probably on 17 March 1926, the same day that his wife also returned home, after having spent some time at a nursing home. He was complaining of a cold in his head and shivered. After dinner he went to bed, remaining there for the following week. Dr Jacob Gavronsky called on Behr on 18 March, following Mrs Behr's concern at her husband's screams. Behr complained of stiffness and spasms in his legs. He could not use his feet. The doctor's examination did not uncover any organic injuries. However, the pains in his back and limbs led Gavronsky to conclude that these were symptoms of some kind of irritation of the central nervous system. Two other doctors were summoned and injections of morphine were given.

Although bronchial pneumonia developed, Behr's condition seemed stable for the next few days. The doctors concluded that he had quite recovered and only needed a little rest. However, on 19 March, Behr had vomited small pieces of orange and water. He also took sleeping tablets and drank brandy.

Behr was not neglected. A succession of nurses was employed over the next few days. Violet Robinson was employed on 19 March. She recalled that Behr complained of pains at the top of the spine. He also suffered from spasms, with intervals of a quarter of an hour. Yet he did not look ill. The next nurse was Margery Cassidy and recalled that he had not suffered from spasms and gave her no account of her illness. From 20 to 29 March, Florence Macknow was responsible for his care. She noticed the spasms, but also the periods of calm and thought he seemed well. However, Behr

Finchley Road. Author's collection

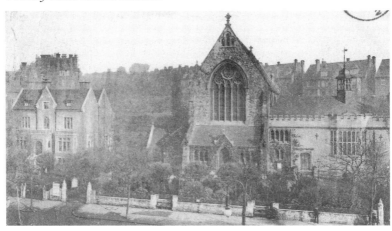

was very nervous about the attacks. Hannah Russ, the cook, thought Behr seemed to be improving.

The illness was seen as being potentially serious. On 20 March, Behr's brother, who was abroad, was sent a telegram to request he come home. He arrived in London on 28 March and visited his unfortunate brother, whom he had not seen for some time. He too thought that his brother did not look ill.

The climax came on the morning of 31 March. Annie Gaffney made a pot of China tea from the tin in the kitchen for the family. She took Behr's cup of tea upstairs to his bedroom. On the landing she met Mrs Behr, who, as was not unusual, took the cup from her and went into the bedroom with it. Tea from the same pot was given to Mrs Behr for one of her sons (she did not see the son drink the tea), but Mrs Behr herself drank hot water. The cups were later collected by Annie. She recalled hearing Behr moaning that morning.

Anna Zabrodoff was summoned by Mrs Behr at about half past eight that morning and she went to the bedroom. Behr was screaming and was clutching the mattress with both hands. These screams were also heard by Ethel, and they woke her up at about eight. She went to her parents' bedroom. Behr called for his doctor and his brother. Anna was then told by Mrs Behr to contact Samuel Behr on the telephone, urging him to 'Hurry, or you will be too late'. Samuel did arrive too late, but Mrs Behr was with her husband at the time of death soon afterwards. By that time, Behr was screaming again and Anna left the room because of that. Ethel also rang for Dr Gavronsky.

Dr Robert Bronte, in the presence of Gavronsky, examined the body. There were no signs of external violence or of any irritant poison. Microscopic spots of blood were examined, as was spinal fluid. After three days he was still unable to ascertain the cause of death. One early opinion was that death was due to influenza.

The inquest began on 3 April before Sir Walter Schroeder, but was adjourned, first to 8 April and then to 20 May, in order to give time for a thorough examination of the dead man's organs. It could then be revealed by Dr Bronte that the real cause of death was strychnine poisoning. Two grains were found in the body, though a quarter of a grain might be enough to have killed him. Anna attested that she did not think Behr took drugs or strychnine.

Detective Inspector Hambrooke and his men had searched the house, but the results had been inconclusive. This was despite finding a variety of bottles, boxes and phials containing drugs in the bedroom. Yet they did uncover a quantity of strychnine in a bottle of gin, which had been placed on a table for the inspector and a colleague to drink. According to Dr Bronte, strychnine tablets might have been dissolved in this gin. A bottle of Endometricitis, with chocolate-coloured pills which contained strychnine, was also found. There had also been enquiries at all the chemists and druggists within 15 miles of Charing Cross to find if anyone connected with the Behrs had purchased strychnine there, but no record of any such purchase could be found. Perhaps it had been bought using an assumed name or from outside that radius.

Summing up, the coroner noted that Dr Bronte had concluded that the poison had been administered on the morning of 31 March. Apparently five minutes would elapse between the administering of the poison and the first symptoms. Death would follow within 20–30 minutes. The only known beverage consumed by Behr on that morning was the cup of tea. If that was the case, then that narrows down the list of suspects to Annie, the parlour maid, and Mrs Behr, and the latter would seem far more likely.

An examination of the will might have revealed a number of possible suspects, namely those who benefited financially from Behr's demise. As said, he was a rich man, whose gross estate was worth £21,260, after death duties £16,260, which was still not a sum to be sniffed at. This will had been made in July 1925. His executors were his brother and one William Ward Higgs, a City solicitor. However, this fortune did not simply pass to one individual as a lump sum. The bulk of it (two-thirds) was divided into four equal quarters, to be held in trust for his four children until they reached the age of 30. They would then receive the capital, which would have been augmented in the interim by interest the sum would have gained. The remaining third was to be invested and the interest paid to a charity, at his brother's discretion, and Higgs would examine the annual accounts of the trust. A codicil granted £500 to Anna Zabrodoff. Interestingly, nothing was left to his wife, who later said, 'I cannot understand why he has left me practically destitute.'

Relations between the Behrs were vexed (though the will was made before the quarrel). There had been a major row between the couple in October 1925. Mrs Behr wished to buy a car in her own name, but her husband refused. According to him, 'she was inclined to be a bit extravagant and fond of a game of cards'. She said, 'He simply behaved like a madman all the time'. Behr even attacked his wife, putting his hands around her neck until Anna arrived, slapped him on the face and he released his wife. In the following month, Mrs Behr, without informing anyone she was doing so, went abroad to Shanghai in order to sell some property of hers there. Due to the political instability there, she was unable to realize her assets, and was forced to request money from her husband. He had sent her the £300 required and so she returned home. Behr met her at Cherbourg in February 1926, laden with gifts. She spent the next few weeks in a nursing home, only leaving on 17 March.

Others spoke of the couple's domestic unhappiness, too. Behr's bank manager claimed the 'deceased had frequently spoken to him of his unhappiness with regard to his wife'. Max Kirschener, a timber dealer and neighbour, said there were quarrels, but that he did not want to leave her and that he loved his family. Yet there was no evidence of any infidelity on either part.

The servants also seemed to think that their master and mistress were contented. Annie Gaffney said, 'Mr and Mrs Behr live happily together ... I have heard of no quarrels or any trouble'. Their Russian governess, despite witnessing Behr attack his wife, nevertheless agreed, saying they 'were devoted to each other ... seemed and acted as though they were a newly married couple'. If his wife was responsible, and she did have the opportunity (the only drink he definitely had was his morning tea), presumably the motive was hatred of her husband or/and the hope of financial gain, assuming that she was unaware of the contents of his will.

Could Behr's death have been the result of suicide or accident? He could either have put the pills in his tea or in another drink which no one else was aware that he had had. He was reported as being depressed and had health worries. Max Zausner, his departmental manager, said that his boss was unhealthy, had stomach pains and had problems sleeping, so took drugs to help him sleep. Furthermore, his brother recalled being told by him, 'If I get another attack as have had I could not stand it any more'. Hambrooke also queried whether this was a case of murder, writing:

> I have been unable to discover any reason why any person should administer the strychnine to the deceased in order to murder him, but on the other hand, it does, at present, seem that he was a man who took drugs and was at times depressed.

On the other hand, Samuel said, 'I know of no reason, from a business point of view, why my brother should knowingly take anything which would be likely to cause his death.' But he did not think it was murder, either, adding, 'I have no reason to think that any person in the house would do him any harm'; and that his brother was 'always a kind man to everybody'. Could Behr have taken the strychnine himself in order to stave off his health problems?

Yet no one was ever formally accused of the murder, if murder it was. Whether his brother knew anything of the affair, his secrets, if any, went to the grave with him in 1942, when he was buried in the Jewish section of a London cemetery. He was certainly comfortably off, with a house on Finchley Road and another in Crowthorne, Berkshire. Behr might have taken his own life, might have taken the tablets by accident or might have been poisoned by either Annie or his wife, and of the two, the latter seems least unlikely. We will probably never know the truth of the matter.

CHAPTER 10

The Murder of a Shopkeeper, 1926

I am afraid as I am being constantly watched

Shopkeepers, like prostitutes, are often in a very vulnerable position as regards criminals. They have something the criminal wants – money – and are often alone in their shop and so are easy targets. Some were attacked and killed. The fictional Mrs Ascher of Andover in Agatha Christie's *The ABC Murders* (1936) was one, as was Robert Venner in New Cross in 1934. And we have another.

Edward Austin Creed managed a provision shop in Leinster Terrace, just off the Bayswater Road. Born in Brentwood, Essex, in 1881, he was employed by Messrs Philip Lowry and Co., cheesemongers and poulterers, and had been for over

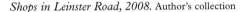

Shops in Leinster Road, 2008. Author's collection

20 years. It seems he was reasonably prudent, with £267 to his name in 1926. Creed was a busy man because he was also a special constable in Paddington. He had been a married man since 1908 and had two daughters. The family lived in Denbigh Terrace, Notting Hill. He seems to have been well respected by those who knew him, with one Mrs Escott saying, 'He was liked by all. I have never heard him speak to anyone who bore him a grudge or was likely to do him an injury.'

As usual, on Wednesday 28 July 1926, the shop closed up at seven in the evening. Maude Rawlings, the book keeper, later recalled, 'I did not notice anyone standing about in the vicinity of the shop when I left'. All the other members of staff left at that time, too. Only Creed and Alfred Leonard, a shop assistant, remained. Leonard prepared some warm water and found a towel for his boss to clean himself up, and then left the premises himself at ten past seven. Creed was not known to have ever entertained people at the shop in the evening. There was no reason why he should loiter there. At half past seven, William Cox, a fellow local grocer, was waiting to meet Creed as arranged. Creed did not arrive. Nor did he come home at the appointed time of eight, and the light in his shop was said to be still turned on at that time. By ten, Mrs Creed began to worry.

At half past ten that night, PC Harry Watts was on his beat in that part of Bayswater. He noticed that the padlock on Creed's shop was missing. Furthermore, there was light coming from a small window at the side. When he knocked on the door, no one answered. Watts could smell gas. With the help of another constable and two other men (John Forbes, a neighbour, and Albert Sykes, a postal worker), he forced the door and they saw the body of a man, lying on his back at the foot of the steps. It was Creed. Watts rang the police station. Inspector Jones arrived and reported:

Upon our arrival at 11.30 pm, I saw two large patches of blood on the floor of the shop about four feet from the entrance. There were splashes of blood on the panels of a side counter on the right hand side of the shop.

There were also marks on the sawdust on the floor, as if something or someone had been dragged along it. Smears of blood were found in the office. Creed had been killed by a blunt instrument between 7.10 pm and about 8 pm and his face and head were covered in blood. He was probably killed shortly after his staff left, because the wash bowl and towel that had been put before him had not been used. He was fully dressed, but was not wearing his jacket and was in his shirt sleeves.

Another clue was a pair of men's old buttonless slip-on chamois gloves. Both were left-handed. One had a gusset in the wrist and the other had a portion of the wrist cut off. Both were dirty and of low quality. There was also a brown coat button on the scene. Unfortunately, there was no trace of any fingerprints anywhere.

Yet another clue lay in the fact that a man had paid for goods earlier that day with a £5 note – a very high denomination indeed and one rarely used to buy goods in a grocer's shop. Given that money was missing from the shop, if the man who paid with this could come forward, he might be able to give the police the serial number of the note, which would help them to track it down and so find the killer. The man never came forward.

The motive for the murder certainly appeared to be money. In total, £51 14s 8½d was missing from the drawers in the office. A few copper coins were found on the floor of the office. John Forbes declared:

> I do not know of any person who bore him a grudge, nor did he ever inform me of any person with whom he was on bad terms. He did, however, complain bitterly of the conduct of street hawkers in Leinster Terrace and the neighbourhood and I know that he, like myself, had remonstrated with them.

Mrs Creed gave evidence about her husband's concerns. He said that he had recently been asked by a former member of staff for a reference, but had refused him. She also referred to another former employee, who had been dismissed in May,

Denbigh Terrace, 2008. Author's collection

because of his slovenly working habits. Her husband had recalled that he had not turned up for work during the General Strike earlier that month and he thought that the man had socialist sympathies, which Creed abhorred. However, Mrs Creed said that her husband did not fear this man. Neither man was ever named.

Albert Sykes recalled seeing a young woman in the street, who asked him if she could have a look around inside the scene of the crime. He refused. She was about 22, with brown hair and a thin face. She told him, 'I have seen two men on the roof about a quarter of an hour ago.' Whether these were the attackers is another question.

There was no shortage of possible leads from a variety of sources. On the afternoon of the day after the murder, two men were seen going into the Moseley Road Baths in Birmingham. Their clothes were dirty. When they left the baths, they were in different sets of clothes. They gave their old clothes to the attendant at the baths and told him to burn them. Examining them, the man found blood on the right leg of one of the trousers. Although this was suspicious, there is nothing to link these two men with the murder. The police tried to trace them, but without any success.

There were other sources of possible assistance. These included two anonymous letters from the same hand. The first was postmarked Notting Hill, 8.30 pm, 4 August, was addressed to 'Inspector' Wensley at Scotland Yard and was marked 'Important, urgent':

> If you make the offer of a reward of £100 or more through the papers and promise me police protection I will tell you where to find and who the two murderers are in the shop murder case. If you keep to Notting Hill you are not far wrong. They know me so I am frightened to do anything but write.

Two days later there was another missive from the same writer, to the same recipient, though he was then correctly titled Chief Constable (having been promoted since the Lechevalier case of 1924). It was labelled 'Personal' and read as follows:

> I shall try to see you on Sunday. I am afraid as I am being constantly watched, I think. I am afraid to go and get a stamp so must post this letter without. If I ring you up and give the name and address you will know who it is writing you.

An appeal was put out in the press for the writer to come forward, but they never did. They were told that if they did not come to Scotland Yard by midday, 14 August, a specimen of the handwriting would be published in the press in the hope that someone would recognize it. By 23 September, the writer, a woman, was identified, but her story lacked corroboration and it was thought that it was it was merely an attempt to have a certain male suspect convicted of the crime and he was already under suspicion. We do not know who this man was.

Another anonymous letter, which was so vague as to be meaningless, was sent by a criminal and read:

> Enclosed is the photograph [*not in the existing police file*] of the Notting Hill Gate murderer. You will find him

somewhere in South Ealing. I can't come forward as I am
wanted myself for housebreaking but I hope you get him the
double crossing rat.

If these leads came to nothing, there were many others. Mrs
Eagle of Colville Terrace found a pair of bloody trousers in a
room which she had let out to John Cropp and his wife, who
had now left. The pair were found in Maidstone. Apparently
Cropp had cut his hand with a knife and his injured finger had
bled.

Ernest Kaye, a taxi driver, recalled having taken a fare from
near Leinster Terrace on the night of the murder to Maida
Vale. The passenger was a man aged about 30, clean shaven,
very fair, of slim build and was wearing a grey suit and grey
trousers. The passenger was never located, but was probably
wholly innocent of murder.

Known thieves also came under suspicion. On 11 August,
one William Mitchell said that he had been with a man called
Albert Southwell, who had been in Leinster Terrace at a
quarter past seven in the night of the murder. Apparently a
woman was heard shouting 'They are murdering a man in
there'. Southwell was questioned by the police, but was
allowed to go. George Peacock and Patrick O'Donnell were
also well-known criminals. They had been in Luton from 19
July to 1 August. O'Donnell had been in Harrow in late
August and had been known to have committed larceny at
Westbourne Terrace, Paddington, on 16 July. In the following
year, James Morant, a thief who had been in and out of the
army in 1918–26, said that one Stephen Turner, a fellow thief,
told him that 'He is now in the run himself over a killing job
in Leinster Terrace, Bayswater.' Ernest Edwards, in 1927, said
that 'Brummy' and 'Lancashire' were to blame. The latter was
Walter Pratt and the former was untraced. He was thought to
be an unreliable witness, in any case.

Louis Valleroni, a 35-year-old married man who delivered
newspapers for a living, had been taking Louise Goodchild for
trips out on his motor cycle, one as far afield as Ruislip. He
was suggested by his erstwhile girlfriend as the killer.
Apparently, after the murder Valleroni was always flush with

money, but refused to go near the shop where Creed had been killed. He said he was not in the vicinity of the shop on the fateful evening and that Louise was a liar.

The police also made house-to-house enquiries in Leinster Terrace, Leinster Gardens and Craven Hill, though only on 28 August, one month after the murder had taken place. They also checked on known thieves in Paddington, Notting Hill, Notting Dale and Marylebone. Quite why there was a delay in such standard procedure is not stated, but it certainly made the questioning less effective. None of the statements taken now survive and so it must be assumed that these enquiries were inconclusive.

There was a fresh crop of allegations in the following decade. One, in 1931, was from Mr Angelo Portinari, who lived near Tottenham Court Road. He said that a fellow lodger came in drunk and talked about the murder. In 1932, Lilian Goodchild, a prostitute, said that Edgar Bidanville, a busker, and Jack Kennedy, a friend, were outside the shop on the night of the murder. Although Bidanville was a minor criminal, he had been employed as a nightwatchman on that night from half past seven. She was thought by the police to be a liar. Another unreliable woman was Mrs Gritton, who told the police in 1936 that a man called Studd was the killer. Yet she was very vague on details, being 'garrulous and unreliable'.

What had probably happened is this. One or two men waited until Creed was alone and isolated, with the door unlocked as the shop manager looked forward to leaving. They probably knocked on the door and gained admittance, as it was said that the obliging Creed would open up for a customer who just wanted a single item after usual hours. They then knocked Creed on the head and dragged the body to the office, which was then ransacked and the money taken. Because the crime was not motivated by any personal animus, the guilty party was not known by any in Creed's circle. Lacking modern scientific methods or DNA, the police had no way of identifying the violent criminal/s who were responsible for the execution of this well-planned and cold-blooded robbery with violence.

CHAPTER 11

The Kidbrooke Railway Mystery, 1929

If you go to 5 Rayner Place an see Mr F. Kallis, he is the man you want

The morning of Wednesday 13 March 1929 began like any other, for Mr John Charles East and his wife, Winifred Maud East, of Gordon Road, Wanstead, in East London. Mr East left at 8.40 to go to work at the Commercial Road, Stepney. He was employed there as an auctioneer and valuer. He kissed his wife goodbye.

The couple had married in July 1926. Although they had no children, they seemed happy enough. Most married women did not work at this time and Mrs East, being no exception, was able to enjoy a certain amount of freedom. She went late that morning to meet a friend, Mrs Margaret Ann Richards of

Bexley Station. Author's collection

Chieveley Road, Barnehurst. The two had been friends for six years and once Mrs Richards had lived near Mrs East in Wanstead. They met at Bexleyheath station at a quarter to midday and then went to Margaret's house, about a mile south from the railway station. They had a pleasant day together there, before going to Barnehurst railway station, so that Mrs East could catch the 7.43 train back to London Bridge station.

The two women arrived at the station two minutes early. Mrs Richards bought a single ticket for her friend to travel to Bexleyheath, for she had only bought a day return ticket from London Bridge to Bexleyheath. The train arrived and Mrs East found an empty third-class carriage, sitting in a corner seat, facing the engine. Mrs Richards later described what happened next:

> I stood at the carriage door talking just a moment with my arm across the entrance to the compartment, and as I stood there, I felt a slight touch on my arm. I immediately let my arm fall and a young man stepped into the carriage and walked to the further end of the compartment. He sat on the same seat as Mrs East, but he sat at the further end. The train started at once.

Liverpool Street Station. Author's collection

Meanwhile, Mr East was making his way to Liverpool Street station, where he had arranged to meet his wife at about a quarter past eight, in order to catch the 8.29 train to Leytonstone and so to go home. She did not arrive. Thinking she might have taken an earlier train, he went home as planned, but she was not there. So he returned to Liverpool Street station and began to wait for her. He met every train from London, but still she did not arrive. Finally, he took the last train home. It was now midnight. Mr East later recalled, 'I then became seriously alarmed and went to Wanstead police station' in case there was any message there for him. There was not, and so he reported his wife as missing. The Wanstead police contacted their colleagues in Bexleyheath. Enquiries there soon revealed that Mrs East had indeed left Bexleyheath as planned.

On the morning of the following day, George Foster was driving the first train out from Charing Cross to Dartford, the 5.34. After passing Kidbrooke station, he thought he saw a body near the line. He contacted his colleagues at the next station, Eltham, and Walter Harling, the Eltham stationmaster, was sent to investigate and took the next train to London to do so. It was at ten past six when Mr Harling found the corpse of a young woman, about three-quarters of a mile from Kidbrooke station. Seeing a policeman, he showed the man his discovery. The corpse had been decapitated. They also found a handbag and a handkerchief nearby, but there was no sign of her hat. Her watch was broken and there was a necklace under her body. An empty purse was also found nearby, but further investigation revealed that this did not belong to the deceased.

PS Ladell from Lee police station was soon on the scene. He examined the handbag and found it contained seven shillings and five pence, and an umbrella. Charles Rye, a railway policeman, was on the same train on which Mrs East had travelled. He found her felt hat, her bank book, a postcard, receipts and two empty envelopes. Under the seat was her savings certificates book. Henry Colegate, the Crayford stationmaster, assisted in the hunt. Inspectors Tabard and Wells had the train removed to Beckenham Sidings for a further search. According to Tabard, 'There was nothing whatever about that compartment that would indicate any struggle. There were no scratches on the woodwork and no glass broken.'

The body was taken to Greenwich Mortuary on Lamb Lane, where Dr Walker, the divisional surgeon, made an initial examination that morning. He estimated that the time of death was not less than six to eight hours before and not more than 12–14 hours. Hence the time of death was between about 5 pm and 1 am. Mr East was called for at nine and when he arrived, he identified the body as being that of his wife.

Initially this seems to have been thought of as a tragic, though mysterious, accident. There were no footprints near the corpse. Railway officials surmised that Mrs East may have been alarmed at something, opened the carriage door and then fell out of the carriage in which she was travelling. The suction caused by the speed of the train would be sufficient to draw her under the train wheels and to her death. The carriage doors would automatically close once opened on account of the wind pressure.

However, an inquest still had to be held and this was opened at Greenwich on Friday morning, 15 March. Tabard and other Scotland Yard officials were present. Yet the only evidence taken by the coroner, Dr Whitehouse, and the jury was that of Mr East. He told them a little about his wife's health and mental state. According to him she had been in fair health – she had had a little heart trouble a couple of years before, but had made a full recovery. At that time, she had spent six weeks in bed following medical advice in order to prevent any kind of breakdown. The couple had then had a three-week holiday. His wife was not depressed, nor was she of a nervous temperament. She had no money troubles or other worries. Mr East told them, 'We have lived very happily together, and she has always been of a cheerful disposition.' He added that he thought that a few pound notes were missing from his wife's possession; perhaps £2–3, as he had seen her with that sum on the day prior to her death. The inquest was then adjourned until 22 March.

Perhaps the coroner wondered if this was a case of suicide? Other rumours were spreading in the press that this was a case of a foul play. Certainly the police were making enquiries and put out a general appeal on 18 March, outlining the basic facts and adding:

> The police are anxious to get in touch with all passengers who travelled from Barnehurst Station to London or intermediate stations by that train on the night in question, and are particularly anxious to get in touch with any person or persons who travelled on the train and who may have any particular reason for remembering the journey. Any information should be communicated to New Scotland Yard or to Superintendent Barrett, Blackheath Road Police Station, Greenwich SE 10.

The inquest recommenced on 22 March. John Bradnam of the railway company's surveyor's department, outlined additional physical clues. He said that the distance between the body and Kidbrooke station was 603 yards. He also produced a plan of the carriage in which Mrs East had travelled. He said her powder puff was found ten yards from her corpse; her handbag was 12 feet six inches away and her handkerchief was 26 feet distant.

Mrs Richards was able to supply further information about the man who entered Mrs East's carriage. Unfortunately, she had no opportunity of taking a good look at him, and no reason to do so either. However, in answer to the coroner's questions, she replied thus:

> I only saw him from the back but he struck me as being slightly built, of medium height and I know he had a cap on … it was light in colour … he was on the youngish side, between 20 and 30. I came to this conclusion mainly from his build and also from the way he got into the carriage.

She added that he was wearing a fairly light coloured overcoat of thick cloth. She did not recall anyone else standing on the platform. However, it had been dark and it was possible that someone might have been in the waiting room, unseen by Mrs Richards. When asked about her friend's mental state on that

Passenger steam train 1920s. Author's collection

day, she said that she was 'quite cheerful and seemed quite healthy'. There was no sign of depression, 'She was most cheerful and in good spirits the whole time she was with me.' She was looking forward to seeing her friend again.

Two of the railway staff were next to give evidence. Charles Witcher, a carriage locks examiner, told that the locks on the train doors were in perfect working order. If the doors were opened between stations, they would close on arrival, as the application of brakes automatically did this. Leonard Debney was the booking clerk at Barnehurst station. He reported that six or seven people boarded the 7.43 train there. He did not see anyone board the train at the last moment though, in contradiction of Mrs Richard's statement.

However, two witnesses heard suspicious sounds and allegedly saw the killer leave the train at Kidbrooke. Miss Lilla Smallwood and Margaret Fleming, a typist, boarded the train at Eltham for the short trip to Blackheath. Miss Smallwood recalled that she heard the screams of children in the carriage next to theirs. Then she heard something smash, and that sounded like glass. The two of them looked out of the window in both directions, but could see nothing. At Kidbrooke, they saw a man leaving the train from that compartment. He banged the door shut and then went to talk to the platform porter. Because of the sounds they had heard, she paid close attention to the man, whom she described thus:

> He was of medium height, broad shouldered and well built, very pale complexion, clean shaven and dressed in a dark grey cap and a dark khaki garment with yellow buttons – the kind of tight khaki garment that officers wore during the War.

The man was aged between 20 and 30. When she left the train at Blackheath (the next stop after Kidbrooke), she looked into the compartment, but could not see anything unusual about it; no broken glass; and they did not alert the railway authorities. They only got in contact with the police when they learnt the following day about the corpse being found. It should be recalled that trains did not have communicating corridors and so the only means of leaving a compartment was at stations. This could be very dangerous as it left passengers isolated.

Margaret Fleming confirmed much of her friend's statement, but thought that the screams had been those of a woman. There was then some discussion about different sounds, with the coroner saying that he thought that the banging of a carriage door sounded like that of breaking glass, but Margaret disagreed. Tabard said that the noise of the train would have drowned out most other sounds.

Margaret gave her own description of the man they thought they had seen leaving the train. He was very pale and with a fair complexion. He was wearing an old grey cap and a long officer's overcoat, which looked old and had leather buttons. At this moment, a grey-haired man, wearing a khaki overcoat and an old grey cap stood up in court and Margaret declared that the man she had seen was wearing these type of clothes. Margaret thought the man looked as if he might be a labourer and that he was still talking to the porter when the train left Kidbrooke. He was not seen giving a ticket to the porter, and Margaret assumed he was telling him about the screams they had heard.

It was now time for William Ford, the Kidbrooke porter, to speak. He said that there was no one on the Kidbrooke platform waiting for the 7.37 train and that he did not issue any tickets. Indeed, he had locked the exit door as the train had arrived. According to him, no one left the train – in flat contradiction to the statements made by the two aforesaid women. Had anyone left the train, he would have seen their ticket or have issued them with one. He did neither. Ford did recall talking to a nightwatchman, who was on the platform with him. He admitted that a member of railway staff might have left the train there without his noticing.

Then the elderly man wearing the khaki overcoat and a cloth cap, who had been pointed out to Margaret earlier, stood up. He was Charles Ford, a nightwatchman employed by Greenwich Council in connection with roadworks near to the station entrance. He went to the station each night for water, usually on three occasions. On the night of the 13th, he had been on the platform when the porter locked the door to the exit. The two men had a chat whilst the train arrived and departed. He agreed with the porter that no one left that train on that occasion.

Dr Arthur Davies of Harley Street had carried out the post mortem. He announced that there were three types of injuries on the body. First, there were many bruises. Some of these were on her arms, some on her legs and some on the front of her body. There were burns on the head, neck, shoulder, thigh and knee. Finally there was the decapitation. The clothing was blood-soaked and the injuries were consistent with being run over by a train, with the burns caused by electrocution. The bruises were caused before death. He concluded, 'she would fall, be electrocuted, and shortly after be decapitated. The bruises were not of sufficient severity to have caused death.' Dr Walker agreed with his colleague on the cause of death.

The coroner then pressed him for an analysis of the injuries. Davies said that he thought the bruises were 'consistent with a struggle, whereby the arms were grasped or knocked by the assailant'. He demonstrated two blows on a court official and added that the two would have been standing up at the time of the blows.

The inquest was then adjourned until 28 March, when it was concluded. It was a short hearing, lasting only an hour and a half. Albert Garr, the train driver on the train on 13 March, was first to give evidence. He noticed nothing unusual on the journey at all, but noted that no inspection of the train had been carried out between Eltham and Kidbrooke. Robert Gow was the train's guard. He recalled that the train was made up of eight carriages. He said that several people boarded the train at Barnehurst and several alighted. A few people had boarded the train and alighted from it at the stations between Barnehurst and Kidbrooke. He had not noticed an open carriage door when he looked out of a window between Eltham and Kidbrooke. When asked if anyone left the train at Kidbrooke, he agreed with his colleagues that no one did, but unlike them he thought that someone had entered the train at that station; probably a man. According to him, 'I am quite sure I saw no one leave the train at Kidbrooke. It would be possible but very improbable to miss seeing anyone.' The train waited at Kidbrooke for about twelve seconds. At Charing Cross, about 50–60 people alighted. He was asked whether it would be possible for a carriage door to be opened between Eltham and Kidbrooke, for a woman to get out and then for the door to be closed again, and Garr thought it was possible, but that it would have to be done quickly, for it was only about a minute and forty seconds between Eltham and where the corpse was found.

Then the man whom Garr had seen board the train at Kidbrooke gave evidence. He was Joseph Colney, a civil servant at the Ministry of Aviation's Aerodrome at Kidbrooke. Whilst he was standing on the platform he did not see anyone talk to the porter, but as to whether anyone did so as he was boarding, he could not be certain. He had been wearing a light rain coat and a bowler hat. He thought he might have seen a young woman in the booking hall on that or the following night, which was unusual. Various other railway and police officials also gave evidence, the essence of which has already been related.

The coroner then began his summing up. He ruled out suicide as a possibility as Mrs East was not depressed or unhappy. He asked when it was that the young man who entered the compartment at Barnehurst left. Although the two female witnesses claimed he had left at Kidbrooke, their statements had been flatly contradicted by the railway staff and Mr Colney. The other question to ask was whether Mrs East opened the compartment door in transit of her own accord, or whether she was pushed out by another. If the former was the case, she might have used the door as an escape from another, and if so, this was still murder. It should be remembered that these compartments did not have communicating corridors and the only means of exit or egress was via the door onto the platform. The coroner did not think it could have been an accidental death, because that did not account for a number of her possessions being found in the compartment. He told the jury they could return an open verdict if they were not satisfied whether this was a case of accident, suicide or murder.

Yet the jury made their decision in five minutes. They were unanimous in their decision that Mrs East had been pushed out of the train or had jumped out in order to escape her assailant. Mr Connolly, the solicitor employed by the railway company, expressed the company's sympathy with the deceased's family, and the coroner thanked the police and the company for their assistance.

The case remained unsolved and was recalled in the local press in January 1931, at the time of the mysterious murder on nearby Blackheath of Louisa Steele (chronicled in the author's *Foul Deeds and Suspicious Deaths in Lewisham and Deptford*).

In *The Hound of the Baskervilles*, Sherlock Holmes, having been told of the facts as expressed in the press, asks, 'This article, you say, contains all the public facts?' To which Dr Mortimer replies, 'It does.' Holmes puts another question, 'Then let me have the private ones.'

For this case, these can be found in the appropriate police file. However, much of this file consists of statements by the witnesses who gave evidence at the inquest and so is already known to the reader. The police hunt centred around a search for the man who entered Mrs East's compartment at Barnehurst. The file contains a number of communications which were made to the police by the public, and these shall now be examined.

One was an anonymous letter, received on 4 April, which read as follows: 'If you go to 5 Rayner Place an see Mr F. Kallis, he is the man you want for Mrs East, between Kidbrooke and Eltham he worse a cote like the soldier he as been in prisen a lot.' Frank Callis was the man named in the letter. He was an unemployed labourer, aged 35, and living in Islington with his wife and two children. He had been in prison for assault prior to 1914 and was known to wear an army greatcoat. Yet his wife said he had been at home on that night by half past seven. The police discounted the letter, believing it to have been written by an ex-landlady of Callis's, who bore him a grudge.

Other men came under suspicion. John Cross, a 36-year-old builder, who wore a khaki coat and worked in Orpington, was one. Yet his foreman vouched for him and Cross said he did not know Barnehurst station. A cleaner in Camden Town said an ex-miner called, asking for a pair of boots, and that he answered the description of the man. Thomas Baden-Powell, aged 25, of Brighton and of independent means, had travelled into London to see his solicitors on the day of the murder – he wore an officer's overcoat. He came under suspicion, too. Bombardier Gun from Preston barracks also thought he saw a man in khaki at Victoria station on the day of the murder. Finally, a man answering the description of the wanted man, was seen leaving Lewisham station on the day of the murder. None of these leads came to anything.

Tabard concluded, on 1 May in his report:

> I beg to report that enquiries have been continued with a view to trace the man who was said to have got into the railway carriage at Barnehurst station, occupied by the deceased, Mrs East, but no information has been obtained that would lead to his identity or throw any further light on the matter.

After the murder, there were calls for greater safety arrangements on trains, such as sliding panels between compartments and special carriages. These were not heeded. One writer later noted that the public had little to fear, for between 1864 and 1929, only seven people had been murdered on trains in England. In fact, suburban trains did not have interior corridors until the 1970s, when rising crime led to them being installed.

Was the young man seen entering the carriage at Barnehurst guilty of murder or was he innocent? If the latter, he presumably left the train before it arrived at Kidbrooke, either at Bexleyheath or at Eltham, and then was understandably reluctant to involve himself in a murder case in which he was prime suspect. If he was guilty he could have left the train after Kidbrooke, because it appears he did not do so there, despite the two women claiming he did. It seems fairly certain that the man they saw was the watchman, who was patently not the young man seen by Mrs Richards at Barnehurst. They probably did not see him alight from the train, because he did not do so, but saw the watchman on the platform and, not seeing anyone else there save the porter, made an incorrect assumption. The motive for the crime was probably robbery, though it may have been an attempted sexual assault.

CHAPTER 12

Did Frederick Field Kill Annie Upchurch? 1931

There was no doubt that this case was going to be a bit of a stinker.

As Spilsbury's first biographer noted, 'The 1930's are particularly rich in notorious cases from the seamy side of life in the West End.' Although the murder discussed here was officially unsolved, there is a strong possibility that the killer was known.

Frederick H L Field, aged 27 and born in Tenterden, Kent, in 1903, was employed as a sign writer by Messrs Hilder & Co., sign contractors of Great Pulteney Street. He was a married man and lived in Sutton. He and his manager, Douglas W L Bartrum, went, on 2 October 1931, to an empty shop premises on Shaftesbury Avenue. They needed to gain access to the place in order to carry out some repairs to water pipes in the flat above. Unfortunately they did not have the keys and the place was locked. However, they were able to force open a wooden door at the rear of the premises on New Compton Street.

Bartrum saw something on the passageway floor and later remarked, 'It looked like a wax model'. His colleague thought that it looked more like a corpse, which indeed was the case. Bartrum told Field to fetch the police, which he duly did. Field found PS Ferridge on duty at Bloomsbury Street and told him, 'Sergeant, will you come round the corner? There's a woman in a shop, and I think she is dead.' Senior officers were soon being assembled and Chief Inspector Sharpe, who was getting ready to go on holiday to the seaside, rang Superintendent George Cornish and demanded his presence at Shaftesbury Avenue. He recalled: 'Well, the hunt had started when I got there.'

The body was that of a partially unclothed unknown young

Shaftesbury Avenue, c.*1930.* Author's collection

woman. She was wearing a green dress, which had been provided by a firm in Bear Street, Leicester Square, and which had been pulled up behind her head. Her silk jumper had been used as a gag. Her watch had stopped at 8.20. From marks on the floor, it seemed that she had been dragged along by the feet for some yards to her present position. Her cloth belt had been used to strangle her. A woman's hat lay under her corpse. Her handbag was missing and there was no sign of the keys to the premises. It was presumed that robbery was the motive, especially after it was stated by Mary Davis, housekeeper at the deceased's lodgings, that she had had £4 in her handbag, as well as a ring and a cigarette case.

Dr Fairlie, the police surgeon, noted the cause of death. He also said that death had occurred about 36 hours prior to when he had seen the corpse on 2 October. There were no other marks on the body and there had been no sign of sexual interference.

It was uncertain at first who the victim was and suggestions were made to the police. Doris Lynn, aged 30 from Leeds and who wore a green coat, was one possibility and another was Miss Elisa Wicks of Farnham. However enquiries revealed that the dead girl went by the name of Miss Norma Laverick (and

Leicester Square. Author's collection

Warwick Street, 2008. Author's collection

others) and that she was allegedly a dancer. From 1930, she worked at Bear Street, but lived at Warwick Street, Victoria, and did not bring men back here. Her real name was Annie Louise Norah Upchurch, aged 20, who had been born in London in 1911. Her father had been a railway employee and she had lived with her parents at Cricklewood until she was

14. Apparently she had caused no end of trouble to her parents, chiefly with young men. She had spent time in a home in Sussex in 1925 and then in a Salvation Army hostel in Norwood. In 1927 she worked as a servant in Euston. Annie left home permanently in December 1927 and became a prostitute in the West End, aged 16. She gave birth to a baby girl, Marjorie Norah, in November 1928, who was looked after by one Mrs Callaway. As one commentator wrote, 'She seems to have been a kindly and likeable creature, as are so many of these unfortunate women whose lives end tragically; the men involved in such cases are uniformly detestable.' One Annie Norman described her thus, 'I always found her to be a very nice girl. She was very kind and good natured.'

Her last known movements were as follows. On 29 September, she left the flat at 11 in the morning. At 2 she went to Bear Street with a man and went there again with another four hours later. Miss Marie Davies recalled having seen her then. It was common for her to take two or three men to her flat each day, but she rarely did so in the evening. She had begun to make her way back to Warwick Street at eight. However, one Foster (and of him, more anon) claimed to have seen her near the Arcade at Leicester Square. Although some prostitutes claimed to have seen her on 29 September and 1 October, the police believed that Foster's sighting had been the last.

As with most murders of prostitutes, it was not going to be easy for the police. Sharpe noted, 'There was no doubt that this case was going to be a bit of a stinker. There was no doubt about it; anyone of hundreds of people might have murdered her and we'd got a tough job ahead of us.'

There were numerous suspects. As the police stated, 'During the course of the enquiry a number of persons have come under notice, who could be reasonably suspected of being the author of this crime.' Peter the Pimp, 'a dark-skinned fellow of Greek extraction', was one. He had been seen by other women watching Annie and there had been quarrels between the two of them over money. However, it transpired that the witnesses had mistook another girl for Annie and so he was ruled out. Other suspects included Geoffrey Cowlan, who had met Annie in July and said they were engaged. She was known to have had made several trips to Chatham, where he was stationed. He was a sailor and a jealous man. He had been spying on Annie and had been keeping watch on her address on 30 September. However, he was at Chatham barracks on the evening of 29 September, having last seen her three days previously. Other suspects were a street costermonger and a man from Zanzibar. Another was William Docherty, a 24-year-old waiter of Wimborne, Dorset, who confessed to stabbing Annie to death (which she had not been), but he was in jail at the time of the murder.

The police investigation, as ever, was painstaking. Apparently a total of 502 statements were taken. Houses in Shaftesbury Avenue, gullies and railway stations were searched for the missing keys and the handbag. They were never discovered.

The inquest took place on 19 November, presided over by Oddie. In the mean time a number of additional facts had emerged. Frank Foster, aged 27, an excellent cricketer and of independent means, of Ryder Street, bravely came forward as an acquaintance of the late girl. On 28 September, he had met her at Piccadilly Tube station at 8 pm. He had said that she seemed lonely, hungry and poor. Foster thought that she was troubled, though whether by a particular individual or by money worries, he was uncertain. He went with her to Warwick Street after they had had dinner at a restaurant. He spent the night with her, albeit with him sleeping in an armchair. According to Cornish's memoirs, Foster claimed that a man came to the door of the flat and asked her how she was. When she said she was fine, he left, but Foster never caught a good look at him. Could he have been her pimp? Foster later gave her a cheque for £10. This was because she told him that she was in debt to the tune of £7 or £8 and he felt sorry for her. Unfortunately, though Foster was expecting money into the account, he had, in fact, less than £10 in it. When questioned about the murder, he denied that he had ever been in the empty shop, did not possess the key and had only heard about the crime on 3 October when he read about it in the newspapers. The police thought he was one of three major suspects, claiming he was 'a man who is fond of the company of prostitutes and possesses a peculiar temprament'. The police thought that his motive was that he had knowingly given her a worthless cheque and he had been the last known person to see Annie alive. Yet there was no evidence to directly link him to the murder.

It was then that the events, real and (perhaps) imagined, of 29 September were recounted. Hilda Mary Margaret Keenan had been employed by a firm of estate agents who were agents for the shop premises in question. It was she who gave the keys to Field on that day so he could do some work there. He duly went there to remove some signboards. Whilst he was standing in the window, he claimed that a man wearing plus fours came into the shop and asked him for the keys. Field initially hesitated, but the man said, 'It's all right. I have an order.' Field was then given a piece of paper on which were the following words, 'Please hand the keys over'. It was signed by the agents. The keys were then handed over. Hilda Keenan told the court that she did not issue such an order.

Shortly afterwards, the man returned. He told Field that he had bought the premises and that he intended to use it as a shop selling fancy leather goods. He wanted some lighting work done and asked Field to carry out the work. He then arranged with him to meet at Piccadilly Circus station that night to discuss the matter. The stranger then said he would return the keys to the agents and departed. They met as arranged at 9.15 pm and Field was advanced £2. On returning to the shop, the man found he had not got the keys, so left Field there in order to find them. Twenty minutes later, Field was still alone. The man never returned.

Four days after the discovery of the body, Field was taken to Richmond Police Station. There he was shown a man in the cells, who was wearing a pinhead striped suit. Field claimed, 'As soon as I saw his face I recognized him as the man I gave the keys to, even before he had spoken.' We shall return to this man shortly. William Finlay, a sign fixer of Kentish Town, recalled that, on 30 September, Field told him that the stranger was a tall man, wearing brown plus fours, well built, with a tanned face and a gold tooth.

Oddie asked Field a few questions. He said that he thought it odd that the two men met at Piccadilly Circus station, instead of going straight to the shop. Field replied that it was the first location which came into his head. He also asked why Field had changed his clothes before meeting the man for the installing lights into a dirty shop; surely best clothes indicated meeting a woman? Field had a reply for this, too, 'The main reason was that I had to transmit business with this man and I wanted to look as decent as I could.'

Oddie concluded that whoever had had the keys to the premises had entered there with the girl and robbed and killed her. The inquest was adjourned until 26 November. Sharpe suspected Field was lying, as 'his story didn't sound too good from the first'. Oddie felt that Field was 'an impudent and self confident fellow'. However, at the conclusion to the inquest, the main theme concerned Peter Webb, the man identified by Field as being the mysterious stranger to whom he had given the keys. Webb was represented by Mr Sharman, a solicitor. Field and Webb were the police's other two main suspects.

Apparently Webb, whose proper Christian names were Harold John, had been arrested by DS Smurdon on 5 October for confidence tricks, and was later sentenced to three months in jail. Among Webb's possessions at Richmond Hill Hotel was a plus four suit in bright check, as well as a £1 note, two 10s notes, 6d in silver and 7d in bronze. The suit was the reason why Field was called to identify him. Oddly enough, though Field identified Webb as the stranger, he did not identify the suit as the one worn. Furthermore, when Field claimed to recognize Webb, the latter said, 'I do not know you', to which Field replied, 'Yes you do. I handed you the keys of the shop in Shaftesbury Avenue last Tuesday.' Webb persisted in his innocence.

Webb was then called upon to give his version of events. He had left Bognor on 28 September and went to the Belmont Hotel, a boarding house in Highbury, where he paid a deposit and took a room there. He was wearing his plus four suit on the following day, leaving the boarding house at 10 am. He had a coffee in Islington and took a no. 19 bus to Kingsway.

Alighting at Aldwych, he met a Mr Couton, a business associate, there and the two walked up Kingsway and had drinks in a hotel. He went to the Tivoli cinema and saw *The Bad Girl*. He left at 3.15 and attended a tea dance at the Regal, Marble Arch. Mr King, the host, saw him and spoke to him. Webb left at 6.05 and then returned to the boarding house. Numerous witnesses, such as Mr Fisher general manager of the cinema, John Hay a waiter at the Belmont, and Mr King, all vouched for Webb's movements. It should be added that Webb did not have a gold tooth. He denied ever meeting Field or going to anywhere in Shaftesbury Avenue or Piccadilly Circus station. Clearly he was not the stranger Field claimed to have met. Indeed, the question arose whether Field had met anyone.

The inquest returned a verdict of murder by person or persons unknown. Oddie was unhappy about the verdict. He thought that Field was guilty and that 'he knew that I knew who had committed this murder'. He noted a number of pertinent questions. Why had Field not taken the stranger's name and why had the man taken possession. Why should the man wish to rent a £1,000 per annum premises and then give the work to a workman unknown to him? Why should the stranger give Field £2 and then disappear? Why did he make the railway station the rendezvous? Why did Field dress so smartly? Why did he not bring any work equipment with him? Oddie thought Field's story nothing but 'a wicked and malicious pretence and imposture'.

Another suspicious circumstance surrounding Field was his finances. He was paid 47s a week. Shortly before the murder, he paid a colleague the £2 he owed him. Just after the murder, he apparently had a windfall, and was able to give his wife some much needed money. It was possible that this windfall had been the money he stole from Annie's body after killing her. Yet this could not be proved.

Field was also thought to have known Annie previously. Florence Taylor said that Gertrude Douglas of Bear Street claimed, 'He used to phone her up nearly every day at 7 Bear Street and I used to take messages.' She thought that Field often waited for her outside the flat. She also offered some

Bear Street, 2008. Author's collection

speculation that on the fatal night 'he took her there on the understanding that he was going to show her a flat'. We cannot be sure if this was correct or why it might be. But all this is speculation.

In the following years there were some confessions. One was in 1932 by a man in prison, but he had made similar confessions before to other murders, and in any case, he had not been at liberty when Annie was killed. Albert Bradshaw, a 51-year-old waiter, and a burglar of Camden Town, claimed to have killed her and confessed at Kentish Town Police station on 28 December 1932, but after being remanded was released. Three years later, Sidney Smith, an Australian and a former soldier, confessed. His alleged victim was not Annie, but was one Florrie Payne, and she was still alive. Yet he could not account for his movements, was mentally defective and had a history of violence. Detective Inspector Edwards, in 1935, thought he might have been guilty.

Another suspect was Captain Alexander Patterson, from New Zealand. He lived in London with a woman and was separated from his wife. Aged 37 he was just over six feet tall. He came under suspicion because he wore plus fours and had a gold tooth, so appeared to be similar to the man Field allegedly met. Although he was not initially found, he eventually was and was cleared. One Captain Bourke was seen in a hotel in Ross on Wye and he also looked like the mystery man. He could not be located.

Other witnesses came forward. A Norwood tobacconist recalled seeing an Asian man in his shop who seemed suspicious. A woman saw an Indian student knocking a woman against railings near Leicester Square. A suspicious man was seen at South Merton railway station by a man who did not want his name to be made public.

But perhaps the most peculiar twist of the tale was the confession by Field at Marlborough Street Police station in 1933. He told the police, 'I want to give myself up for the murder of Nora Upchurch at the empty shop in Shaftesbury Avenue.' This was because he thought his wife and child would be better off without him. He signed a statement and was formally charged with the offence. Part of the confession read as follows:

I had tea, washed, and dressed myself, and returned to the West End. About 9.30 I was in Leicester Square, when I saw a girl whom I afterwards knew to be Norah Upchurch. Neither of us spoke then, but at about 10.25 that night I saw her in Bear Street, Leicester Square and she beckoned to me from across the road. I went over and asked if she could come back to my place and she agreed.

After they arrived at the empty shop, he said that she bit him:

When she hurt me I lost my temper and grabbed her around the throat. She seemed to faint and fell back out of my hands to the floor. She did not speak or murmur. I knew something serious was wrong when she fell back and I lost control of myself and cannot remember what happened afterwards. I stayed there a few minutes and surmised she was dead before I left.

On taking the handbag, he was concerned his fingerprints might appear on it, so he threw it away in a ditch in Sutton. Sharpe spoke to him and was convinced he was guilty. After speaking to him, he recalled, 'It's a funny feeling, sitting with a man whom you realise is a murderer.' Cornish, however, may have been less convinced, as he does not point the finger at Field in his memoirs, and indeed noted: 'The murder of Norah Upchurch was to prove one of the most baffling which I have had to handle.'

Field was sent for trial at the Old Bailey. What emerged was very strange indeed. It was found that, on 25 July that year, a newspaper office had told the police about Field's confession. It seems that Field entered into an unorthodox arrangement with them, agreeing to confess if they would give him an undisclosed sum of money. At the trial, he pleaded not guilty and, apart from the confession, there was nothing else to show that he was guilty. He was therefore acquitted.

Mr Justice Swift was unimpressed by the turn of events and issued a stern rebuke:

Anything more disgraceful I have never heard. A man goes to a newspaper office and says, 'I am confessing that I have been guilty of murder'. The newspaper representatives thereupon take him about the country, photographing him, and for hours refrain from communicating with the police as every decent and respectable citizen ought to do as soon as he hears that a crime has been committed. ... I warn newspapermen of these proclivities, that if they do this sort of thing, they are likely to find themselves very seriously dealt with.

When Swift had asked Field to explain his behaviour, Field answered, 'I wanted the whole thing cleared up properly. The whole thing was left in the air. People said "This man has done it". I could not turn round and say, "I have been proved innocent". I could not do anything or say anything.' The judge replied that it was 'a peculiar way of proving your innocence to say you are guilty'.

As an epilogue to this story, one Mrs Beatrice Sutton, a Clapham prostitute, was found strangled in her flat, in April 1936. Field, who was now in the RAF, confessed to the crime, as before, then, as before, retracted his confession. This time, though, he confessed too much, revealing information that only the killer would have known, and the jury found him guilty of this murder. He was hanged.

Whether this is proof that he killed Annie as well is impossible to know. The circumstantial evidence is strong and the fact that he employed a similar technique a few years later is also highly suspect. Certainly officialdom, in the form of Sharpe and Oddie were convinced of his guilt, though they were writing after the second murder. Cornish, writing without this knowledge, did not venture such an opinion. The truth of the matter will never be known for certain, however.

CHAPTER 13

Violation and Murder in Notting Hill, 1931

There have been many theories advanced by various people to the identity of the murderer of Vera Page, but although we continued our investigations with all possible energy, the murderer has never arrested. (Superintendent Cornish)

Those who remember the 1930s often recall how safe the streets were in comparison to more recent times and that children could walk about unmolested. Whilst generally this was true, in this shocking case it was not, and though this case is the exception that proves the rule, it makes it even more terrible. The young victim had been molested as well as murdered, and furthermore, her violator/killer was never convicted. Oddie wrote, 'To my mind the most revolting of all crimes is the murder of little children by sexual perverts.' This is probably the least unknown crime of this book, but previous accounts have been limited in their detail and have not used all the available evidence. This account is both fuller and reveals new evidence against the principal suspect.

The western suburbs of central London were a curious district and were described thus in 1952, just before the grim revelations of Rillington Place, where at number 10 eight people were killed between 1943 and 1953:

that very mixed region of London which stretches north from Shepherd's Bush and Holland Park to Wormwood Scrubs and to the Harrow Road. It is a region where the shabby-genteel mergers into the slum, where the police used to patrol Notting Dale in pairs, and where, on the other hand, miles of mean streets are fringed along the south by avenues of trees and pleasant squares, expensive flats and large houses with drives, a colony of studios and the woodland of Holland House. It is one of the few hilly districts north of the Thames, with Campden Hill and its water-tower standing up over against the similar sharp rise, topped by another landmark, the spire of St. John to Evangelist, up which Montpelier Road climbs from Clarendon Road to Ladbroke Grove and Lansdowne and Stanley Crescents.

Before examining the crime, we must first introduce the principal characters involved in it. The little Page family consisted of three members. There was Charles William Page (born in Fulham in 1892), a painter employed by the Great Western Railway Company. Isabel was his wife (born in 1895, née Essex), and they had married in the summer of 1918 in London. Their only child was Vera Isobel Minnie (born in Hammersmith on 13 April 1921). They moved from Chapel Road to a house in Blenheim Crescent in January 1931. Also living with them was Maud Essex, Isabel's 23-year-old niece

Blenheim Crescent, 2008. Author's collection

and her boyfriend, Harry Lovatt, aged 24. Vera's grandmother and aunt lived nearby.

As with many working-class people in this era, they did not occupy the whole house, but rather lived in rooms in part of it, in this case, on the ground floor. Other occupants were Arthur Orlando Rush, a 71 year old who had once run his own florist's shop in Kensington, and his wife, Annie, who was one year his junior. After living in Charlotte Terrace and Hesselway in 1891 and 1901, respectively, by 1931 they had lived in Blenheim Crescent for at least 20 years and occupied the top floor. They had been married in London in early 1891 and a few weeks later, their first child of at least four was born. This was Percy Orlando. He was the only one who was still living with them by 1920. In 1921, he married Daisy Lilian Wheeley, who had been born in Kensington in 1890. The newlyweds lived with his parents until about 1925. Then, the young couple who were childless began to live in the three rooms at the top of a house in the nearby Talbot Road, and Percy visited his parents once or twice a week, letting himself in with his own key.

Talbot Road, 2008. Author's collection

It is deeply to be regretted that we do not know what the relations between the two families were, nor what they thought about each other, or even how the different family members interacted with each other. It certainly seems that both families were close knit.

Vera, who was 10 years old by December 1931, was four feet seven inches high and attended the nearby Lancaster Road School. According to her mother, 'She was very shy in front of strangers, and not likely to speak to them. If she knew anybody, she would speak to them.' On the afternoon of Monday 14 December, she came home from school as usual. Then she left home to visit her aunt, Mrs Minnie Maria Essex, who lived a few minutes walk away on the same street (about 200 yards away). Vera was wearing black shoes, stockings, a blue gymslip with black braid, a blue jacket coat and a red woollen jersey. She also had a red beret. When she left home, her clothes were clean. Her mother reminded her not to be late home, for her tea was being prepared for 5.30 pm. Vera needed no second warning as she was hungry and wanted to eat.

Vera arrived at her aunt's house at 4.30 pm. She collected her school swimming certificates and carefully put them into a large envelope. She then began her short walk home, at about 4.45 pm and was apparently eager to get home. Yet, despite her hunger, she walked past her house. She was next seen, by the 12-year-old Charles Hewett and the 13-year-old Irene Stegman, looking into Taylor's, a chemists' shop at the junction of Portobello Road and Blenheim Crescent at about 5 pm. Vera liked looking at the Christmas gifts displayed there, especially the soap in the shape of dominoes. A man and a woman were also standing outside the shop (we do not know their identities). At 6.30, one John Barden, a ship's steward, said she was looking at a shop window. It is unknown what she did in the intervening hour and a half. Fifteen minutes later, Robert Ritches, a salesman, saw her in Montpelier Road, walking in the direction of Lansdowne Crescent. He used to know her, having lived in the same house as the Pages for nearly two years. He recollected that she had her beret and her certificates. That was the last time she is known to have been seen alive. Yet Ritches was seen by the police as an unreliable witness, 'a shifty individual', who had been convicted for embezzlement eight years ago' and so they thought he may not have seen her.

Vera certainly never returned home. Her parents and neighbours began the search for her that evening and continued on the following day. All Vera's relatives were visited, but to no effect. They had her reported missing at Notting Hill Police station at 10.25 pm. The police took the matter seriously and acted promptly. On the following day, her description was circulated among the local police and the women police were also notified (their role was seen to be among children and women, of course). By the evening, the press had been given details, too. Broadcasts were made on the wireless, one stating: 'it is feared some harm may have befallen her'.

Meanwhile, Kathleen Short, who lived in a house in Stanley Crescent, found a red beret outside the property at 9 pm on Tuesday 15 December. She evidently took it into the house

Stanley Crescent, 2008. Author's collection

and put it to one side. She also found scraps of paper and swept these up without looking at them. These may have been the remains of the school swimming certificates, which were never found. These items had not been there that afternoon.

On the morning of Wednesday 16 December, Mrs Margaret Key of Goldhawk Road, Shepherd's Bush, was on her way to work. It was 6.40 am. She was walking along Holland Park Avenue in order to get to Shepherd's Bush. At the junction with Holland Park Gardens, she saw a man crossing the main road, from Addison Avenue, and walking southwards. He was wheeling a coster's barrow, in which a large bundle was covered by a red cloth with a knitted fringe. She proceeded on her way to work. Men pushing coster's barrows were not an uncommon sight in Notting Hill.

At 9.50 that morning, there was a major development. Joseph Smith, a milkman, was making his rounds near Holland Park. He was delivering milk to Silwood, a large house on Addison Road, which is just south of Holland Park Avenue and is a continuation of Addison Avenue, which is north of the main thoroughfare. This was about a mile and a half from Blenheim Crescent. The house belonged to the wealthy widow of Charles Smith, who lived there with three servants. The milkman had previously been to that house at 5.30 am, to make his deliveries to the tradesmen's entrance, when it had been dark. At 10.20 pm, on the previous day, Mrs Smith had returned home, leaving at 7.50 am the next day, and saw nothing unusual. By ten to ten, on 16 December, it was light, and Joseph Smith, making his second delivery there, made a most terrible discovery. He saw a pile of earth and leaves. These partially concealed the corpse of a little girl. He recalled:

> The moment I stepped into the garden. I saw the body. The child was lying on her right side, and the lapel of her coat almost covered her face. She looked as if she were lying asleep under the bushes, except that her face was like marble. I told the cook at the house, and then went out and found a policeman [PC Wager].

Addison Road, 2008. Author's collection

Wager contacted Notting Hill Police Station and they rang Paddington station. Here were Superintendent George Cornish, one of Scotland Yard's 'Big Five', and Detective Inspector Mallett. They went to Silwood and there found the body of Vera Page. She was fully clothed, though lacked her beret and her certificates. There were a number of clues. First, there were spots of candle grease on her clothes. Secondly, there were traces of coal dust on her face. Thirdly, and perhaps most important, in the crook of her right elbow was part of a bandage and lint, which had been on someone's finger. Finally, there was a smell of ammonia on the bandage. Unfortunately, after a search of the grounds, no other clues could be found. It was deduced that the corpse could not have been put there before early that morning, as it had rained the night before and the body was dry.

Dr William Kirkwood, the divisional surgeon, was called and arrived at 10.20 am. Spilsbury carried out a post mortem at 4 pm. The cause of death was manual strangulation. She had also been sexually assaulted before death. Spilsbury was uncertain when the child died. He thought that death occurred 'Not very long after the child was missing, I think on Monday night.' He also noted that the body was warm and that there was some decomposition. He deduced that the corpse must have been kept in a warm place, perhaps inhabited rooms in a house, rather than a coal cellar or outhouse. Marks of a cord were found around Vera's neck after death, too, perhaps it had been used as an aid for carrying. We do not know whether Vera was given a meal by her killer or their accomplice (if any); there is no surviving record of the examination of her stomach contents which must have been made (as it was with a child murder in 1914). This would have been an important clue and it must be regrettably assumed the report was discarded.

Meanwhile, that evening, Kathleen Short found a partially used candle near her house. She brought this and the beret to the attention of the police. The beret was identified as being that of Vera's and it was noted that there was paraffin on it.

Vera's father told of his distress, 'She was our only girl, a fine little lass and I could not imagine anyone wanting to do her harm. She was full of fun and life, and was the joy of our hearts.' There were also tributes from her schoolfriends and teachers, who described her as a popular girl, being bright and fun. The mental strain proved too much for his wife, who fell ill soon after the discovery of the murder. So much so that a policeman was stationed outside the house to deter any callers. However, they received many sympathetic letters from people from all over the country, many of whom were complete strangers.

The murder investigation could now begin. Cornish took command and Mallett was another key detective in the case. About 200 detectives were assigned to the task. They issued a statement which was published in the press on 17 December, briefly stating the known facts of the case and encouraging anyone who had seen her or had seen anything suspicious to come forward. As usual, the police were painstaking in their investigation and over 1,000 statements were taken (none of these now survive – documents being weeded routinely). Sheds, garages and unoccupied flats were searched. Photographs of the victim were also distributed to jog people's memories. They also questioned all the usual local suspects: men with known 'indecent tendencies'.

At least three such men were questioned at Ladbrooke Road Police Station. One was a labourer, who spent an hour with the police. Unreported (by name) in the press, one of the three was the forementioned Percy Rush. He was interviewed by Mallett at Notting Hill Police Station on 18 December. He was 'a short thick set man with a fresh complexion, and wears horn rimmed spectacle. He has thick black eyebrows and a heavy moustache.' Although we know little about his family life, education and career, there are a few pertinent facts. Like many young men, he had volunteered for military service during the Great War. He had been a private in the King's Royal Rifle Corps 1914–20, though his military career was apparently inconspicuous. By 1931 he was aged 40 and had been employed at Whiteley's Laundry, Avonmore Road, Olympia, as a flannel washer for two years, and was described by a colleague as a workmate, rather than as a friend. More pertinently, he had been convicted of indecent exposure in 1923 and 1927, receiving a month in prison for each offence. Between 1929 and 1931, a man answering his description had been reported as exposing himself to various women, including Rose Napper and Queenie Marshall at Rosemead Road. Although he was picked out of an identity parade and charged at West London Magistrates' Court in January 1932, he pleaded not guilty and was discharged. It is worth noting that in June 1931 he had exposed himself to two schoolchildren, or in the words of a newspaper, 'behaving indecently with intent to insult females'. He was seen as suspicious in the locality, too, 'His conduct for some time past in the neighbourhood has been the subject of much local gossip.' It was claimed that Rush had been seen loitering about the neighbourhood in the evening, having been identified by his attaché case which contained his lunch. Rush denied he ever went about at night without his wife, but did admit that he did sometimes loiter on his way from work.

His lodgings were searched and his clothes taken away for testing in the laboratory. The results were certainly interesting. Semen was found on his coat, as was coal dust. He could not explain the presence of the former. It may have been a result of his 'flashing' or could have resulted from a violent sexual crime.

One crucial clue was the bandage and lint. These smelt of ammonia, a substance commonly used in laundries and indeed it was used at Rush's workplace. Rush had recently injured the little finger of his left hand at work (about two weeks before the murder); there were two sores there. He said he had made a rough bandage for his finger at work and once home, his wife made a better one, with their domestic supply. This was so the ammonia at work would not irritate the cut. However, he claimed that he had thrown it on the fire on Friday 11 December, in order that the fresh air might heal the wound and so was not wearing it on the crucial Monday 14 December. His workmates, when questioned, thought that he might have been wearing it on Monday, but they were uncertain. Dr Roche Lynch examined the bandage found with Vera's corpse and wrote, 'After the examination of photographs, examination by ultra violet light and other tests I have come to the conclusion that the lint and the bandage forming the finger bandage are different from the samples found at Rush's house.' The bandage was thought to fit Rush's injured finger, but again, this was not certain. Others were questioned who had injured fingers, but none lived in the vicinity of the murder. Enquiries were made at hospitals and to doctors and chemists about anyone who had been treated for an injured finger.

The police searched Rush's rooms. Rush carried a pyjama cord around with him, allegedly to keep his trousers up. This could have been used to make the marks around Vera's neck. Then there was the question of the paraffin, the coal dust and the candle. A paraffin rag was found in his flat and they had a coal cellar; Rush took coal from the cellar to the house and so his clothing would naturally bear traces of coal dust. Hundreds of thousands of other households had coal cellars, so the coal evidence is hardly conclusive. Candles were not uncommon in homes of the time, too, and Rush's had some. The paraffin rag had apparently been there for months and was used for cleaning the stove. Although a red table cloth was found there, similar to the one seen by Mrs Keys over the barrow, it was shown to the witness and she did not think the two were one and the same. The colour was the same but the fringe was different. She also failed to pick out Rush from an identity parade on two occasions, though her initial description of the man she had seen was not unlike Rush.

Rush was questioned about what he knew of Vera. He often visited his parents, at least once a week and often more (he had visited them on Sunday 13 and Thursday 17 December). He had a key to the house. As said, Vera had lived in this house since January 1931. According to him,

> I knew Vera Page. She was a pretty sweet little kid. I liked her. I always looked upon her as a nice little girl. I have never given her sweets, money or toys. I have seen her playing in the streets outside her own home, I last saw her about three weeks ago.

He said he recognized her picture in the newspaper. Yet later, he claimed, 'I have seen her and have only said good evening to her' and would not have recognized her in the street. How well did he really know her?

He gave an account of his movements on 14 December. He had been at work in the daytime, starting at about 8.30 and taking a lunch break between 1 and 2. He left work at about 5.55 pm (though we only have his word for this), but, knowing his wife was visiting her mother on that evening, and not wanting to be at home by himself for long, decided to walk home and to take a longer route, arriving home much later than usual. Normally he would have caught a bus to Notting Hill Gate and then walked home. Instead, he bought collar studs from Woolworths, leaving there at 7 pm. He walked along Kensington High Street, looking at the contents of shop windows, then went up Church Street to Notting Hill Gate. Rush then walked up Kensington Park Road, which took him near both Stanley Crescent and Blenheim Crescent. He arrived back home at 8.15; his wife was there and they went to bed at 10.45. He did not visit his parents on this day or the following, though he normally did so on Monday or

Kensington High Street, 2008. Author's collection

Thursday). On the following Tuesday, he left work at the same time and travelled by bus to Notting Hill. He reached home at 7.15 and remained there for the rest of the night, so he said. He said that he could not have got out of bed without his wife knowing it. No one was ever called upon to verify his statements about his movements.

Another question was the location of the murder. Could it have been in the coal cellar of the house in Stanley Crescent where the beret and candle were found? The cellar door was unlocked (the previous tenant, Thomas McDougall O'Connor, who left on 9 December, had taken away the padlock with him), so was accessible to anyone. Furthermore, the Short family, who now lived there, played gramophone records in the evenings and had the wireless on at full blast. Experiments showed that they would not have heard Vera scream had she been there that night. Yet the body would have had to be stored in warm rooms after the killing, because the corpse's decomposition was relatively advanced.

The inquest was opened at Paddington by Oddie on 18 December, but was adjourned. The coroner was enthusiastic to bring it to a successful conclusion, later writing of his 'fixed determination to spare no effort which might lead to the discovery and apprehension of this terrible monster'. Rumours in the local press initially suggested that a motorist, a small, dark young man, wearing a black overcoat and a bowler hat, had abducted and killed her. Apparently he had been offering sweets and toys as an inducement to children, whilst driving around the streets in a small saloon car. Another rumour was that Vera had been seen riding the handle bars of a bicycle, ridden by a well-dressed man, with a black moustache and a scar on his cheek. Yet it is rare for a stranger to have committed crimes of this nature and these theories were soon discounted. The police made a search of neighbouring garages and sheds. A few days later, an Underground official gave rise to a search being made at Holland Park tube station. Vera's funeral took place on 23 December, at the Presbyterian Mission Hall (where Vera attended Sunday School) on Kensington Park Road. The Revd Guthrie said 'There is nothing I can say to you who mourn in bitter sorrow, except that your grief is being borne today by the whole nation.' Four days later, many people visited her grave at the newly opened Kensington Cemetery in Gunnersbury Park. Police attended the service and the burial, suspecting that the guilty party might have been there, too.

Kensington Cemetery, 2008. Author's collection

Several women claimed that they heard Vera just before she was killed. Oddie made a reference to a deaf woman who claimed she heard a child's voice in Rush's rooms on the 14 December. However, he added, 'This lady was deaf and may therefore easily have been mistaken.' Two women who lived in a flat in Ladbrooke Grove, opposite Stanley Gardens, said that on the same night, at about 8.30 pm they heard a scream, 'It was the scream of a child in pain'. They could not, however, see anyone from across the road. As one declared, 'There was not a soul in sight. It was most eerie. This sudden single shrill cry coming through the night.'

Another witness said that he had noticed rather odd behaviour on the early morning of 15 December, on Montpelier Road. There was rustling in the bushes in the front garden, and then he saw a man running in the direction of Clarendon Road. This may not have had any connection with the murder, however, but was probably a would-be burglar.

Inspector Neil thought that the killer was either a maniac or/and insane. He noted that 7,000 people were released annually, apparently cured, from asylums, but he thought that some remained dangerous. With this case in mind, he asked the rhetorical question, 'What do the police know of the mental history of the male population in and around the densely populated neighbourhood in which little Vera Page was done to death?' It is unclear, though, whether the killer was insane as well as evil.

The police investigation was grinding to a halt. Detective Inspector Emanuel wrote on 18 January 1932:

> So far, some thousands of statements have been taken, and every channel explored to trace the murderer, but unfortunately, up to the present, we have not met with success, and indeed our only suspect in this case is Rush. Intensive enquiries are being continued in every direction, including special attention to Rush and the possibility, even now, of finding some person who saw him on Monday 14th in company with the dead girl, or under circumstances that would strengthen our suspicion of his being the person sought.

In public, they were upbeat, referring to new clues and a man being strongly suspected.

Despite that, the adjourned inquest was resumed on 10 February. The witnesses and evidence were presented to the jury, but their inconclusive nature was also pointed out, too. Rush elected to give evidence. He stressed that he was wholly innocent, that he barely knew Vera and had not been near Blenheim Crescent, Stanley Crescent nor Addison Road on 14–16 December. He described his movements and said that he had not seen her on 14 December. He now said that he had very little knowledge of Vera and had only spoken to her once. He claimed he would not know her again, despite being pressed on this matter by Oddie. At one point, when being asked about the bandage, he began to show signs of stress, drumming his fingers on the witness box and then smiling at the questions he was asked. This earned him a rebuke and he denied he was laughing. On being asked if he had seen her on 14 December, he was adamant that he had not and swore on the Bible to that effect. During his statement, a woman stood up at the back of the court and said 'That man is telling lies.' Unfortunately, we do not know who she was or on what grounds, if any, she made such a remark. After a balanced summing up, when Oddie told the jury that they must be very sure of the evidence before coming to their conclusion, the jury retired for five minutes and then returned to declare that this was a case of murder by person or persons unknown. The jury were not reminded of Rush's previous offences (though they could have read in the local press about his recent appearances at the West London Magistrates' Court) or that there was semen found on his coat, but they did know of his loitering at nights. Oddie then passed on his sympathies to the grieving parents.

Oddie concluded: 'the most interesting and horrible inquest I ever held was brought to an unsatisfactory termination'. He did make some tentative conclusions. First, that Vera knew her killer, that he probably enticed her to a house with the promise of a meal and there he fed her and probably killed her after the meal. He hid the body in a warm room, and then in a coal cellar. The corpse was carried through the streets on

Wednesday morning. The beret, candle and certificates were thrown away on the night after the murder. He had three questions. These were, where was Vera between 5 and 6.45 pm? Why did she walk past her house when she was hungry and knew she could have a meal there? Finally, who gave her last meal?

The other question to be asked is why were the beret, candle and certificates found in Stanley Crescent? The murder probably took place elsewhere, because there were traces of paraffin on the beret and the beret had probably picked up paraffin in the killer's room. But if so, why take the risk of throwing the three clues out as a separate trip, presumably on his way to or from work? Why not dispose of them and the body all together? And why did he tear the certificates up?

Another mystery is Rush's wife, who was never named in the proceedings and is rarely referred to. There is not even a reference to her being questioned about her husband. If Rush was guilty, then he almost certainly concealed the corpse of Vera in his rooms. If so, she could hardly fail to notice the corpse. Was she an accessory after the fact? Presumably she was. The idea that a woman could be involved in such a heinous crime would have been, at this time, inconceivable, but with our greater knowledge of women being involved in child murders (e.g. Myra Hindley and Rosemary West), we know that this is sadly not the case. Another, even more disturbing possibility is that she may have played a more direct part in her husband's crime by giving Vera a meal between 5 and 6.30 pm on 14 December when Vera's whereabouts are unknown. We don't know what her movements were on the day of the murder, so this is, of course, speculation. She, and her husband, could have been perfectly innocent. Yet the police did think that someone was shielding the killer and a woman was used to decoy the victim, and a little girl is more likely to have gone off with a woman than a man.

The police investigation continued. Mrs Key told them on 30 March that she had seen Rush with the barrow, whereas earlier she said she had not been certain. Cornish dismissed this, claiming 'She is too unreliable to take serious notice of.' The official police report admitted on 26 April:

I beg to report that this enquiry has been followed up in all possible directions but unfortunately we have not been able to obtain the slightest information which would carry this matter further. Since submitting last report, nothing of note has come to light worth mentioning.

Mr J A Duncan, MP for North Kensington, asked the Home Secretary whether the suspects would be tailed, but this was not to occur, despite a continuing investigation. Cornish certainly wanted to catch the killer – he wrote: 'if ever a man deserved hanging, he does'. Yet the police were not convinced of Rush's guilt. The case remained open for decades, but had effectively ended in 1932. There were many other leads given to the police from 1932 and for the next 20 years. Cornish recalled that there were letters by theorists, spiritualists and others, giving help, but as the superintendent wrote, there was 'nothing of any practical value'. One Snarey, a convict in Cardiff prison, wrote to say he had relevant information, but on investigation it was found he had not and only made such comments in order to be transferred to another jail. A Chelmsford prisoner said he had seen a man at Birmingham prison who he thought was responsible. Mrs Roth of Cricklewood told police that she had seen a gardener with a cut finger, but did not know who he was. Some of the information sent was downright odd. One Thomas Rance of Camberwell, on 20 April, said that a stranger gave him a tennis ball with the words 'Vera Page' on it. Others accused men they disliked. In 1933, one Mr Alexander accused his new brother-in-law, Henry Hill, of the killing, as he had begun to grow a beard shortly after the murder, had a vile temper and was heard to 'express his intention of strangling other children'. Yet Alexander's motive in telling the police this was that he hated his sister's husband. A report in the *Daily Express* on 25 August 1932 claimed the police had fresh evidence, in this case and that of Louisa Steele (murdered on Blackheath in 1931). Yet this was wholly unfounded and merely served to distress the mothers of the two murdered girls (at least the killer of Miss Steele had, unbeknown to the public, been incarcerated for life for another murder).

In 1943, an anonymous telegram was sent to the police: 'Beware the phantom found Holland Park Road, London, 12 years ago the child Vera Page'. John Howell, who was serving in the Navy, was accused, and the police suspected that his estranged alcoholic wife, who lived in Edinburgh, might be responsible. Mrs Howell admitted this, and as the police noted, 'She has drinking bouts and does these silly things whilst under the influence.'

Interest in the murder continued after 1945. Neville Heath (1917–46), who murdered two women (one of them in a hotel in Notting Hill), was accused of being the murderer, yet as he was only 14 when Vera was killed, it seemed impossible. A letter was sent in 1955 by Thomas Harrington, a convict, implicating two men because he had had a quarrel with them and wanted to get them into trouble. William Muir, 'a victim of confused thinking', wrote in the following year about the murder and was the last one to do so.

Mrs Short, who had found the beret and candle, faced other issues in August 1932. She and her family were given notice to quit from their lodgings and were unable to find new accommodation. She considered changing her name so no one would associate her with the murder. She had had no idea that her actions would have had such consequences.

Yet none of the information sent to the police was taken seriously. The principal suspect remained Rush. Was he guilty? There was certainly a great deal of circumstantial evidence against him. He was in the vicinity of the murder when it happened, he had known the district for much of his life and had no alibi. He had a record of sexual offences. He had recently worn a bandage and one had been found with the victim. He knew the murdered girl. There was also a degree of local suspicion against him. He could have seen Vera on the day before the murder, when he was at his parents, and have arranged to meet her on the following evening after work, when he assaulted her, killed her, hid her in his rooms and then wheeled her corpse to the address in Addison Road. His wife may have assisted him after the deed was done or aided him beforehand. Writers discussing the Ripper murders have accused many blameless men on far less evidence, but in this case, most seem unconvinced about Rush's guilt, though they did not know all there is to know about him.

Yet it could not be certain that he was responsible, for he had not been seen with Vera on the night in question and much of the other evidence is inconclusive. Where did he find the crucial barrow, for instance? No one is known to have reported one missing, or to have lent/sold one to Rush, and one was not found abandoned or in Rush's possession. Could he have borrowed one from work and returned it shortly afterwards? Laundries used them to convey clothes from and to their clients. Yet there is still certainly room for reasonable doubt. It was right that he was not charged, for this was a hanging offence, but the question mark over his guilt or innocence must remain. The killer must have been a man who knew Vera to an extent, if it was true that she did not speak to strangers, and he clearly had a peculiar sexual kink. Killers usually commit lesser offences before they carry out the ultimate crime of murder (John Christie was responsible for several minor crimes before turning to serial murder, as was Arthur Salvage, a double murderer of 1931). He also lived locally and had a bandaged finger. Rush had all these characteristics, but there may have been someone else in the neighbourhood who also did, but who never came under the police's radar, or under any local suspicion. No one else is noted as a suspect, but that does not mean that Rush was guilty of such a heinous crime.

In more recent times, there has been much more study on the topic of child abuse and murder. The conclusions reached are that the perpetrator is almost always someone known to the child. They have usually been getting to know the child (and their family) for some time before the attack/s, gaining their confidence with sweets or toys, and spending time with them. They are usually cunning as well as cruel. Rush would certainly meet this profile, but there might have been others. There are references in the West London Magistrates' Court to other men who we would now term 'sex offenders'. Yet a child's social circle of adult friends is usually limited and no one else was mentioned. It is presumed that a member of the Page family was not the perpetrator of this foul deed, though family members have been known to commit such acts. No one seems to have investigated this possibility at the time, and there seems to have been no psychiatric examination of Rush, either. Had he stood trial, there would have been. Modern forensic methods, too, would have been able to have conclusively proved whether there was a link between Vera and Rush, based on the relatively copious physical evidence. Yet these techniques were sadly lacking in 1931. This may have led to a vicious killer escaping the price of his crimes.

The postscript to the story is that the Pages, having spent Christmas with relatives in Hammersmith, moved away from Blenheim Crescent in 1932, leaving the foul associations of the district behind as best they could. Charles Page died in 1959, aged 67 and was buried with his daughter. Rush's father died in 1933. As to Rush himself, he remained at Talbot Road until moving in 1947, though his wife died in early 1937, aged only 46. His mother lived with him for the remainder of her life, dying in 1944. We know little of Rush's later years, except that he is not known to have committed any more crimes. Rush clearly was not sensitive to his surroundings, nor felt any social pressure/hostility to move away. Was this evidence of innocence or callousness? In any case, he died in obscurity in the autumn of 1961 in the Ealing district. His guilty secrets, if any, died with him. But if he did not kill Vera, who did?

Perhaps the final words should be the epitaph on Vera's gravestone, flanked by angels:

In Loving
Memory of
VERA
BELOVED CHILD OF C. AND I. PAGE
PASSED AWAY
14TH DECEMBER 1931
AGED 10 YEARS
GOD GAVE THE TREASURE FOR A WHILE
TO FILL US WITH HIS LOVE
AND THEN HE TOOK HIS DARLING CHILD
TO DWELL WITH HIM ABOVE.

CHAPTER 14

The Most Dangerous Game, 1932

The unsolved murder of Dora Alicia Lloyd is a perfect short story with the night life of the streets around Piccadilly Circus for its background. (Superintendent Cornish)

The oldest profession is also one of the most dangerous for the practitioner, as they inhabit a no man's land just outside the law. Serial killers often make them their prey, as in the East End in the late nineteenth century (Jack the Ripper) or in the 1940s and 1950s (John Christie), or perhaps as happened in the London of the 1930s (see Chapter 17). Yet in this period, it was the seedy West End, not Whitechapel and Spitalfields, that was the scene of foul deeds. Thorp wrote 'It is unfortunate, but true: The West End of London spells VICE'. Killers could easily escape because they came and went in great secrecy. They rarely revisited the scenes of their crimes, either before or afterwards and usually had no previous acquaintanceship with the victim, so could not be connected to them in any way.

Dora Alicia Lloyd had had seventeen convictions at Marlborough Street Police Station for prostitution from 1919 to 1928. By 1932 she was a widow, as her husband, Walter Lloyd, alias Walter O'Brien, a music hall artiste, had died in 1927. She was described at that time thus:

aged 44, 5 ft. 3 in. or 5 ft. 4 in. in height, very stout build, full round face, dressed in brown dress, black velvet coat, trimmed dark fur at bottom and collar, small black tight-fitting hat, light coloured stockings, probably light coloured shoes. She was carrying a folded newspaper and a small parcel wrapped in white paper.

However, she was said to look younger than her real age. She spent the early evening of Saturday 20 February 1932 in her

Piccadilly Circus at night. Paul Lang's collection

lodgings in Lanark Villas, Maida Vale, with one Helen Herbert, drinking port. At half past ten they left together. Soon afterwards, Dora was in the company of Margaret Marsters, an old friend of 20 years' standing. They had two drinks each at Noah's Ark, a pub on Or Street. They left at eleven, taking a bus to Piccadilly. They then went to Heppell's, a well known chemists for a 'pick me up' (in *Brideshead Revisited,* similar concoctions were purchased from Heppell's for Charles Ryder and friends to help them sober up).

The two women took a bus to Oxford Circus. Dora bought a newspaper there and then they returned to Heppell's. They then went to a cafe in Shaftesbury Avenue for a coffee and parted at Air Street at one in the morning. Margaret recalled Dora's parting words, 'Ta-ta, cock'. There were other women in Air Street, also touting for business. One was Florence Crocker, who recalled a man approaching her. He was aged 35, five feet nine tall, of medium build, darkish, with dark hair and was clean shaven. He was wearing horn-rimmed glasses, a blue melton coat and a black trilby. According to Florence, 'He spoke in a very nice and gentlemanly manner.' However,

Regent Street, 1920s. Author's collection

he was unemployed and could only offer Florence fifteen shillings (which seems a very reasonable fee), so she told him to go home. Apparently he may have lived in Kensington or Wimbledon. Florence said that she would know him again. Margaret James said that the man said hello to her and that he was slightly drunk.

Yet not every woman was so choosy – or greedy. Dolores Blandford recalled that Dora got into a cab with the man whom Florence had rejected. Dolores agreed with Florence's description of him and added that he was of slim build. The police were later very sceptical about the evidence of these women, 'Their statements as to times therefore are none too reliable', coming as they did from 'low type prostitutes and sodden with drink and "pick me ups"'.

Meanwhile, at Lanark Villas, another lodger, Alexander Fraser, a 28-year-old unemployed motor driver, had returned home at ten to midnight. Unable to sleep, he sat up reading. He heard the sound of a car stopping outside the house, followed by a noise on the stairs, a knock at the door and a man's voice. A few minutes later he heard a gurgling sound, followed by several thumps. Silence followed, then the street door was banged and he heard the sound of footsteps in the street of someone walking away.

Fraser took no action until the following day, when he informed the landlady, Mrs Haddock. She did not know anything about the events her lodger described, but the two knocked on Dora's door and then, when there was no response, opened it. The gas light was still burning, so the scene was all too easy to see. Mrs Haddock fainted when she saw what was in the room. They called the police.

PC Charles Wrighton arrived at two in the afternoon and, after noting that Fraser 'seemed very agitated and upset', as well he might, described what he saw in the room: 'I saw the dead body of a nude woman lying on her back; her face was bruised and bloodstained. Her left arm was lying across her chest and the right hand was resting on the right groin.'

Dora's corpse was lying on the bed; the bed clothes were disarranged and her clothing was on the table and on the floor. There was a ten shilling note, a handbag, a mirror, a handkerchief, three pawn tickets and a newspaper on the floor, too. These pointed to the fact that the motive for the crime was not theft, and also that Dora was short of money. A preventative (a sheath) was also found. There was only one possible clue – a pair of dark suede gentleman's gloves which were found lying on the chest and which Helen Herbert said were not there on the previous evening. The room was photographed and checked for fingerprints. Although fingerprints were found on the mirror, these were those of the deceased and Helen Herbert's. Detective Inspector Mallet was in charge of the case.

At half past two, the corpse was examined by Dr Alex Baldie. He put the time of death as being about twelve hours before. He noticed that there was bruising on the forearm and right hand of the deceased, which had probably been caused as Dora tried to defend herself. The face was also bruised and bloody. The cause of death was manual strangulation. Spilsbury later examined the corpse.

A few other facts emerged about the dead woman. She often moved address and had only been renting the bed-sitting room in Lanark Villas since 28 January 1932. A neighbour said she was absent-minded, and once went to the adjoining house under the impression she lived there. She was often known to frequent the West End in the early hours. She had a son, Charles, who had been brought up by his uncle in Cardiff. He had not seen his mother for some years and, ironically, had recently joined the Bristol Police Force.

Dora's fellow lodgers could shed little light on her life and death. Fraser did not know her at all. Walter Powderham, a 29-year-old labourer, had been drinking on the evening of the murder and had arrived home at about midnight. He had apparently slept soundly and heard nothing.

Using Dora's diary, the police tracked down a number of Dora's male acquaintances. One was Frederick Cole, aged 56, of Porchester Terrace. He was a married man and of poor physique. He had met her several times in 1930 and had paid her for her services on each occasion. He had met her after then, though only for drinks. He ended his acquaintanceship with her because he felt it was 'morally wrong to associate with

Porchester Terrace, 2008. Author's collection

her'. He had returned home on the fateful Saturday between 10.30 and 11. The police could not find any marks on his clothes and thought he was 'a foolish old man', physically incapable of murder.

Then there were two others. One was Walter Sandford, a retired engineer, who had briefly lived with Dora in March 1931. He had not seen her after April 1931, he said. This was despite Dora trying to renew the acquaintanceship in January 1932. Henry Grain, aged 61, a lawyer, had had some business dealings with Dora when she tried to convince him that her late husband had been a freemason and so she was entitled to money from them. He had last seen her on 13 February and had told her that her chances was non-existent.

All these men were ruled out of the list of suspects. None met the description of the man seen with Dora as all were far too elderly. The police believed that the killer was a man who, before the morning of the murder, was a complete stranger to Dora.

Helen Herbert also told the police what she knew. She said that Dora read *The Matrimonial Post* (this was the newspaper found in her room, which she had purchased earlier that night). This was so she could write to all the old bachelors who advertised there. She also wanted to extract more money from Frederick Cole, especially as she was not making much money by streetwalking. Another female acquaintance alleged that Dora had told her that she was afraid of a man who used to knock her about. Alas, this man was not named.

It was thought that the killer might have been a regular frequenter of prostitutes in Piccadilly, as he 'seemed to have been familiar to several of these girls who had seen him about the district before'. Indeed, when one man persuaded a drunk woman to take him to her flat, the taxi they entered was surrounded by women, who told the taxi driver that the man was the killer. The man went to a police station, but was cleared because his description did not meet that of the wanted man.

Although no one saw the killer leaving the cab or Lanark Villas, several other people came forward with evidence. On 26 February, cab driver Albert Corbett said that a passenger, one Monica Moroney, told him that her fellow passenger was the killer. A man with a bloody hand was seen on a train from Redhill to Reading on the day of the murder. He was five feet six inches tall, with a red face, grey hair and grey gloves. William Dunlee, who sold newspapers in Westbourne Grove, recalled a man approaching him on the morning of the murder, telling him that he had had a tussle with a woman who had tried to rob him. The man was aged between 35 and 40, was between five feet six and six feet tall, of medium build and was wearing a dark overcoat and a cap. The doorkeeper at the Salvation Army hostel on Old Street was asked to vouch for one James Mackenzie who frequently slept there and told the police that the suspect had not been absent that night. None of these leads led anywhere.

Following the lack of success, there was a conference at Scotland Yard on 24 February between Cornish, Mallett (who were both still investigating the murder of Vera Page, too), the Assistant Commissioner, Norman Kendall and Chief Constable Ashley. They concluded that the cab driver was crucial and put out the following statement:

The police are anxious to trace the driver of a taxi cab, who is believed to have picked up Mrs Lloyd and a man at the corner of Air Street and Regent Street, W., about 1 o'clock in the morning of Sunday last. The cab, which came from Regent Street, drove away in the direction of Oxford Circus, and was probably dismissed at Lanark Villas. The driver is requested to communicate with Paddington Police Station (telephone, Paddington 0661) at the nearest possible moment.

The Cab Driver's Guild also put out a similar request in their journal. No one came forward, however, to either request, doubtless because they did not want to be mixed up in a murder inquiry.

The adjourned inquest was concluded on 7 April. Nothing conclusive emerged from it, except to state that this was a case of murder, caused by person or persons unknown. Oddie, the Westminster coroner, later noted, of the killer, 'No doubt he is still wandering about the West End streets carrying this dreadful secret and probably awaiting the next insane impulse to kill.' He added, 'it is only on the rarest occasion that the perpetrators of these murders by unknown casual visitors to prostitutes living entirely alone can be discovered'.

It seems clear that the killer had no personal grudge against Dora. He went in search of a prostitute and, having found Dora, went back to her lodgings with her. He proffered money (a ten shilling note) immediately. She prepared, almost at once, for sex, having removed all her clothing. Then, for whatever reason, he had a radical change of mind. Perhaps he felt a sense of moral outrage against Dora, and perhaps himself, that he could only assuage by murder. Perhaps it was unpremeditated, for he had not brought a weapon with him. Or perhaps he had a general hatred against women or prostitutes in particular. Possibly he hated one woman in particular, but was unable to kill her with impunity and therefore killed another instead. As soon as he had killed her, he left the house in a hurry, leaving behind him his gloves and the money. He was certainly an angry man, as Cornish commented, 'It is a curiosity that he did not creep out of the house ... he left noisily and walked away like a man in a furious temper, his footsteps echoing along the street.' His identity was never established and the police never had any firm suspects. Had the cab driver come forward, he might have been able to provide more information, but even so, this probably would not have added much to that given by the women of Air Street. His name and address would still have been unknown and almost impossible to ascertain.

144

CHAPTER 15

The Croydon Mystery, 1932

Don't let them try and work anything on you, son

Apart from the mysterious poisonings in Croydon in 1928–9, there was another, even more baffling, murder case which occurred in the town in the inter-war years. Mr Ellis Dagnall was a 72-year-old playwright and actor who lived in a house on Addiscombe Road, Croydon. He had starred in *Who's the Lady?* at the Garrick in 1913. He employed Miss Susan Emberton, aged 56, as his housekeeper. Miss Emberton had been born in Salford in 1877, and her father had been a boat builder. In 1901 she was employed as a servant in Salford.

Dagnall had decided to sell the property and had a sales notice put outside. He left home on Friday 18 March 1932 at 10.45 am to see his daughter, Mrs Dorothy Penley, who lived

Addiscombe Road, 2008. © John Coulter

in Southampton Row, London. Although he had anticipated returning between 7.30 and 8 pm, he did not arrive home until about 9.10. He was surprised to find that the house was in darkness, because his employee was there and a light was usually on in the hallway.

Opening the front door, he entered the house, switched on the hallway light and found a suitcase in the hallway. He had never seen it before and it contained most of his silverware. Inside he found the place in a state of disorder. The drawers in the sideboard in the dining room had been opened and were nearly empty. Clearly, there had been an attempt at burglary, 'I was then sure we had had burglars and rushed to the telephone in the lounge and after a little delay got through to the police.' Two officers arrived and searched the house.

Although the suitcase full of silver remained, other items of value had been taken. These were a small cash box with silver, a pair of gold cuff links, a diamond scarf pin and a gold watch. The total value of the goods lost was £177 and a further £15 in cash had also been taken. Descriptions of these goods were later circulated to police stations over the country. Meanwhile, the silverware which had not been taken was tested for fingerprints. None were found, save for those of Miss Emberton. As the police report noted, 'There was therefore no clue of any description that could assist in establishing the identity of the authors of the crime.' There was no evidence of a break-in.

There were other clues. Mrs Penley later found, when she was tidying her father's house, a dark-brown button in a pool of blood in the back bedroom. An ancient police truncheon was found in the house, which was a possession of Dagnall's. This had been used to sinister result.

Worse was to come. The unconscious body of his housekeeper, wearing her day clothes, was found lying on a bed on the first floor, and she had been hit on the head, which rested on a pillow. Dagnall declared, 'My God. It is my poor housekeeper, Susan. They have tried to kill the poor soul.' Dr Dorothy Day lived next door and her advice was sought. She advised removal to hospital as soon as possible. The injured woman was taken to the local hospital, where efforts were made to revive her. Dr J R Crumbie, the Resident Medical Officer, noted two head wounds; one on her crown and one in the back of her head. However, the doctors were unsuccessful and she was unable to make a statement about her attack. Miss Emberton died at Croydon Hospital on the evening of Sunday 20 March.

The police theory, in public, was that a gang of men who were operating in the locality were responsible. They gained admission to houses by pretending to be representatives from the post office telephone service. They may have visited Dagnall's house, perhaps using this tactic or possibly claiming to be interested in purchasing the house. There had been many callers there previously, and perhaps some had been 'casing the joint'. The housekeeper had been given permission to show anyone who called around the place, if they seemed respectable. Apparently she was not afraid of being alone with strangers in the house. It was surmised that Miss Emberton had returned from a shopping trip and had been struck down by one of the gang, who were panic-stricken at her return. They then fled, leaving the suitcase behind.

Windmill Road, 2008. © *John Coulter*

A couple of witnesses described suspicious figures. Miss Amy Barge saw a young man at the door to the house at 5.20. Mr W H Davies saw a woman leaving the house. She was aged between 25 and 30, about five feet eight inches in height and was good looking. She looked flustered and was rushing towards East Croydon station. Yet, as we shall see, neither of these witnesses was accurate.

One possible clue was that various papers which had been taken from the house – insurance policies, Dagnall's will and a property deed – were found on the following day in a public toilet in Windmill Road, Croydon. This was a mile from the house and 'situated in the worst district in Croydon where most of the local thieves reside'. It was also rumoured that a blue saloon car was used by the criminals, and indeed one had been stolen in Shoreditch on the day of the murder. Yet it was found again at 6.48 pm in Shoreditch on the same day, so this car could not have been used in Croydon two hours later.

Dr Henry Beecher Jackson, the Croydon coroner, began the inquest on 25 March. Mrs Alice Hall, aged about 57, a widow of Stretford, Manchester, and the elder sister of the deceased, identified the corpse. Mrs Annie Brockhill of Stafford House, Upper Kensington Lane, had known Miss Emberton for between 30 and 40 years. The two had once lived together, and Miss Emberton had been her servant for 15 years. On 9 March 1932, the two had gone to the theatre and the now deceased woman had then seemed to be in good health. She was not known to have any male friends. Dagnall had employed her as housekeeper for seven or eight years. He had never known her to be in poor health. She was also able to save £108 15s 7d, which Alice Hall received after the will had been proved.

The inquest was concluded on 8 June. Another clue was produced – the truncheon with bloodstains on it. Yet there was no proof that it had been used against the victim. Possibly she had used it against them. The thieves had shown some respect to their victim, by placing her on the bed. Although the police had made strenuous efforts to find them, they had apparently failed to discover their identity. The verdict could only be wilful murder by person or persons unknown.

Yet the police thought that they knew who the guilty party was, though they did not disclose this to the public, because the evidence against their suspect was minimal, at best. One Mrs May had passed Dagnall's house at five to six on the day of the assault. She saw two men being admitted to the premises. One was tall, wearing a dark waistcoat, a hat and carrying a small case. The police put much store by her evidence, claiming, 'Mrs May seems a sensible woman and there appears to be no reason to doubt her statement.' At six, one Mrs Overton had seen Miss Emberton at the corner of Cherry Orchard Road, going into central Croydon to do the shopping. However, she was not known to have visited a single shop.

One of the men was identified as Alfred Philpotts, aged 25, but already an experienced thief and a professional housebreaker, who had spent time in Oxford prison in 1931. On 28 April 1932, he was sent to Wandsworth prison for 21 months for burglary committed in Kensington and Finchley. On searching his father's rooms, they found a small case which was Philpotts's, and there were indentations inside it which suggested that metal objects – stolen goods – had been stored therein. Philpotts had been seen in Norbury (not too far from Croydon) on the morning of the crime by Detective Inspector Morrish and the policeman picked him out of an identity parade. Dagnall thought he had seen someone like Philpotts knocking at the door of his house two days before he was robbed, though the man he saw told him 'It's the wrong house'. Yet he could not pick Philpotts out from the identity parade.

Philpotts was allegedly told by his father, 'Don't let them try and work anything on you, son.' The young man was quick to assert his innocence, 'I did not enter – Addiscombe Road, Croydon, on the night of the 18th March or on any other date. I do not know where it is.' Furthermore, he had an explanation as to his movements on the night of the crime. Apparently he and William Baldock and another ex-convict had gone to Battersea to rob a bank messenger. This story did not convince the police, who argued, 'It is significant that Philpotts should have an alibi on the tip of his tongue as soon as he is spoken to about this offence, and he puts up his alibi before he has taken the trouble to deny the offence.' The police, as much as they were convinced that they had found their man, had to admit 'There is not at the moment any real evidence against him.'

There were other accusations, as in every unsolved murder case. One was two years after the murder, when George Ford accused Morris Herman of the crime. Albert Norris was also accused by an anonymous letter writer. Yet Norris was in Watford when the murder occurred and the police suspected that the writer was Violet Graham of Hornsey, who had once lived with Norris and, following his departure, wanted to get him into trouble. No further action was taken against either man. As the police report concluded, 'Nothing however, has so far come to light that has caused me to alter my opinion that the information received on the night of 29th March 1932, to the effect that Alfred Philpotts and another were implicated in the crime, is right.'

It was also believed that Philpotts's accomplice was a man called 'Mush'. This man was identified as Jack Rogers and was arrested on 27 May 1932. Yet he claimed that he was stealing from the mayor of Ealing on the evening of the Croydon crime. Another man was identified as Mush, too. This was James Fox, but he claimed he knew nothing of the murder and was at Harringay races on the night in question.

Yet another suspect was William Browne, who was a known criminal. He had robbed and attacked Mrs Jackson at her house in Wickham Road, Croydon, on 22 February 1932. He was subsequently jailed for burglary on 25 July that year. He said he could not recall his movements on the night of the crime, but thought he might have been playing whist with his girlfriend's family that evening. Miss Bramma, his girlfriend, corroborated his story. The police concluded, 'We are satisfied that he was not in any way implicated in the murder.'

The police conclusion was as follows:

Enquiries have been continued into this case and I have kept in touch with informants but no further evidence has been collected against Alfred Philpotts and the man known as

Mush with whom he has assorted at the time of the murder has not been traced.

It is impossible to know who killed Miss Emberton. Philpotts may have been guilty as the police suspected. But as they admitted, there was no evidence against him. The two thieves clearly had not had murder on their mind when they went to the house in Addiscombe Road, as they went unarmed, and one of them probably used the truncheon found there to assault the unfortunate housekeeper as she interrupted their crime. They must have thought they had a clear passage once Miss Emberton let them in and then left the house to do some shopping. However, something made her return home before visiting any shops. Perhaps she had suspicions of her own and thought she could deal with the situation, and she was a confident woman – unfortunately for her.

CHAPTER 16

Whose Body? 1935

We were able to tear the sack open, and then we found a body inside.

Murder automatically creates one mystery. Who was responsible? But in some cases there is more than one question of identity. Who has been killed? There were several cases in the nineteenth century in which bodies, or parts of them, were found in London. They were never identified and their killers went equally unknown. Sometimes it is difficult enough to find the killer, but if the victim is unknown as well, then the task can become well nigh impossible, and deliberately so on the killer's part. To render a corpse unidentifiable means disfigurement or dismemberment, often because otherwise the link between killer and victim would be all too obvious, at least in the mind of the guilty. Their disposal, though, also presents problems, for if they are placed or buried somewhere which might associate them with the killer, then the latter has failed. Therefore, an anonymous location is often chosen, such as a river, canal, a train or a railway station. In 1934, two corpses had been deposited in trunks at Brighton railway station and perhaps that gave the murderer/s in this chapter an idea of how to dispose of their victim.

Just before 2 pm on 25 February 1935, James Eves, a carriage cleaner, was about his work on the recently arrived train from Hounslow into Waterloo. He discovered a parcel wrapped in brown paper, measuring 20 inches by 9 inches, under a seat in a third-class compartment and then went with it to the lost property office. He said to his colleague there, John Cooper, 'Have a look at this. It moves at one end – feels like toes to me.' They examined the parcel and found it was blood-stained. Inside the parcel, within a layer made up of pages from Sunday newspapers, were a pair of human legs, from the knees down. They contacted the railway police at once. PC James Mullin was the first to arrive.

The train had left Hounslow at about 1.20 pm, and had been the stopping service, with stops at Isleworth, Brentford, Kew Bridge, Chiswick, Barnes Bridge, Barnes, Putney, Wandsworth Town, Clapham Junction, Queen's Road and Vauxhall (the same route as that taken by Elizabeth Camp in 1897, when she was bludgeoned to death by person or persons unknown, a case recounted in the author's *Unsolved Murders in Victorian and Edwardian London*). The journey usually took about 36 minutes. There were so many stations at which miscreants could get on and alight. The coach in which the remains were found had been in service all the morning on that same circular route. It was removed to the Durnsford Road sidings at Wimbledon Park at about 7 pm that day. These were strictly guarded until the police could complete their examination, which was led by Chief Inspector Donaldson. He asked other police stations in the district to keep a look out for the rest of the corpse.

It was soon found that the legs were probably those of a man, perhaps aged between 20 and 50. Death had probably occurred very recently. Spilsbury was also called in. There were no marks on the legs. The shape of the toes suggested that the man had been wearing tight-fitting footwear. The man might have been about five feet nine or ten inches tall, judging by the legs. The limbs, however, had been severed after death;

Train leaving Waterloo Station, 1926. Author's collection

possibly as recently as two days prior to their discovery. The cutting had probably been carried out by someone with anatomical knowledge.

Bloodstains were found on the floor of the railway compartment where the parcel had been found, and this flooring was cut away and taken for further examination. Detectives also examined the wrappings as well as the remains inside them. The newspaper in which they were enclosed was a *Daily Express* of 21 September 1934 and another one for 20 January 1935. Part of the front page of one of the newspapers had been cut away by a sharp knife, perhaps to remove a potentially incriminating name or address.

Railway staff along the route were also questioned. Ewes recalled that the compartment in which the parcel was found had been occupied by a working man in his forties, about five feet eight inches tall, but apart from the coincidence of him sitting in that compartment, there was nothing to connect him to the parcel. In any case, he was only noticed by Ewes because he had just entered the compartment ready to travel on the train and, had he been responsible for the parcel, he would surely have left as soon as he could. Left-luggage rooms were searched. A locked dressing case at Waterloo was

Waterloo Station. John Coulter's collection

examined, though it contained ordinary belongings only. A pair of gloves was found on a train at Chertsey, and the stains thereon may have been blood.

Railway staff at Hounslow station recalled seeing a group of three men there at about 1 pm. One of these was carrying a brown parcel and it was he who boarded the train, the others seeing him off, shouting 'So long'. It was believed that these men were Welsh miners. Thomas Soane described the three:

> I think all three of these men would be about 27 to 30, one of them was wearing a brown suit and I remember that his right trouser leg was very much frayed round the bottom. I think they were clean shaven, but of unkempt appearance.

Llewellyn Williams, the ticket clerk at Hounslow, described the man who bought the ticket as aged 22 or 23, five feet ten, clean shaven, with ginger hair and wearing a brown suit and a cloth cap. He also recalled that one of his companions said 'You'll find your way from Clapham Junction to Charing Cross allright.'

Could these have been the wanted men? Or was it a coincidence that one of them was on the same train at the same time as the gruesome parcel?

There was a sequel to the story. In the following month, on 19 March, four Brentford boys, Peter Emptage, Ronald Newman, John Dean and Fred Smitheman, were playing by the side of the Grand Junction Canal near Brentford, whilst on their way to Green Pond to look for frogspawn. Whilst at the canal, they watched a rat swimming and then they saw a sack following a barge. As the sack floated by the canal bank, they used sticks to remove the sack from the canal and examined it, being seen by William Webb, a bargemaster, who also recalled seeing the sack by a lock on the canal. One of two men who passed by remarked to the lads, of the sack, 'Little boys like you should be put in it'. Peter Emptage described their discovery thus:

> I did not know what was inside it, but we thought it might have been a pig or something like that tied up. We were able

to tear the sack open, and then we found a body inside. I was frightened and ran for a policeman. I could not find one, and so sent another boy on a bicycle to Brentford to Brentford police station.

Frank Heath of Southall was also a witness to the discovery and he recalled:

I heard shouts and on looking over the embankment saw a policeman climbing the slope leading to the towing path. There were four boys on the towing path and half in the water was a large sack with one end open. I hurried down and joined the policeman and saw that inside the sack was the trunk of a man. I could see that the head had been severed. The arms had been cut off at the elbow. From the shape of the body the legs must have been severed at the thigh.

Reporters and photographers rushed to the scene, before more police arrived and maintained a rigorous guard, until Donaldson arrived. He had the body removed to the Brentford Mortuary, which was a 'grim little building' in the council depot beside burning slag heaps.

It was a human male torso, which included the upper arms; the lower arms being cut off at the forearm in the same way as the legs had been dissected. Spilsbury concluded that the torso was part of the same body as the legs found at Waterloo. He also found a number of long female hairs on the torso, which certainly did not belong to its owner, nor to those who found the corpse. Another question concerned the location of the rest of the body, which was presumably disposed of after the legs had been found. There were some injuries to the torso, perhaps caused by a barge knocking against it. There was no sign of cause of death.

The wrappings which surrounded the trunk were also investigated, but to little avail. This part of the corpse was wearing a brown woollen vest. It had been made by Harrott & Co., of Aberdeen, a firm of hosiers, who had also sold them in London since 1932. The sack was one of Ogilvie's, flour merchants from Montreal, whose London agents were located at Fenchurch Street. This particular sack had been made in Canada in 1929 and had once contained flour.

Initially it was thought that the sack might have been thrown from a train crossing the bridge over the canal, presumably by the same man or men who concealed the parcel with the legs on the same train. Experiments were made to see if this was feasible, but it was concluded that, though possible, such an act was difficult. Furthermore, the possibility of a heavy object floating upstream was unlikely. It was, perhaps, a very local crime: a piece of paper in the sack had the word 'ford' on it.

In order to find the rest of the body, the canal was dragged with nets and detectives walked along the banks to search the canal using long poles. This took several days, but produced nothing positive. A curved dagger was unearthed, but it was thought that this had nothing to do with the crime.

As ever, a number of messages were sent to the police following their pleas for assistance. Some were anonymous, such as one which alleged a corpse had been buried near an allotment on Ditchling Road. Another said the victim was a man engaged to marry a 26-year-old Irish girl near Brighton,

Acton Town Station, 2008. Author's collection

and had been killed by a young married man of a good social position from Withdean, near Preston.

Anyone seen with a brown parcel became an object of suspicion. William Bashford, a chauffeur at Whytetleafe station saw a man with a brown parcel at 6 pm on 24 February. The man was aged between 28 and 30, five feet eight, with a dark complexion and clean shaven. He had broad shoulders and dark brown hair and was wearing a fawn-coloured overcoat and had a grey trilby hat. He took a train for Victoria. Edward Linegar, a Willesden hair dresser, saw a well-spoken man, with auburn hair, who seemed in a nervous condition on 27 February. He had been using a washing basin and there was a bloodstain on his trouser leg. Two coloured men were seen at Acton Town station with suitcases. A man with a brown parcel was seen on a bus at Aldgate. And there were many other men spotted with brown parcels at this time.

Carl Eric Alven, a surgeon of Cambridge, also came under suspicion. He had left the country in March and applied to join the French Foreign Legion. Hs wife could not recall his movements between 21 and 25 February. The police went to Dunkirk to question him. He had had injuries on his hands which suggested he had been recently involved in a fight. He was also found to carry a scalpel, though as he was a surgeon this is not too surprising. Alven said that he left home because of 'domestic trouble'; not with his wife, but with his father-in-law. He declared that he was in London on 27 February and a friend had given him a knife there. He said the marks of his face were the result of his sparring with a friend outside a pub.

There were also suggestions and queries about the victim, too. Alfred Johnson told the police about Laurence Lenton, a female impersonator, who had once asked him for a pair of special shoes in 1919, which might well have caused the pinching of the feet. Frances Beaumont went to see the remains in case they were those of his father, and concluded they were not. Walter Beaumont, aged 42, of Palmer's Green, had disappeared on 31 December 1934. He was depressed and had become involved with a desperate crowd. Alexander Andrews of Coulesdon reported that his son, the 25-year-old

Frank, who had been employed as a bank clerk until 15
February, had gone missing.

A more pertinent observation was made in the *Middlesex
Independent*, but again, it merely pointed out the difficult
nature of the problem, rather than offering a solution:

> The difficulties the police have to face in this case are many
> – not the least being Brentford's large section of that might
> be termed 'floating population'. These are men who are
> working or have worked on the roads and in factories who
> live in lodging houses and are difficult to trace. It may well
> be that the victim came from amongst that section of the
> population.

A few items which might have been clues were unearthed,
but probably were not. William Charles Witts found male
clothing in a parcel in a Brentford allotment. These were
socks, a top shirt and an undervest. Charles Jones found a
knife at the junction of Finsbury Park and Endymion Road,
possibly dropped by somebody from a passing car. He took
this to Hornsey police station. Two days after the trunk was
found at Brentford, a head was found in a rubbish dump at
South Ealing, yet this turned out to be a false lead, because on
medical examination it was found to be that of an animal.

Three people claimed they had other relevant information.
John Kettle of Hounslow reported on 24 February he had
heard a gunshot. Marjorie Dudley, a schoolgirl, said that she
saw a motor boat near Barnes on 28 February, and the men in
it put something over the side. A sack was seen in the canal by
the Fox Pub, Hanwell, on 17 March. Perhaps a more relevant
witness was a woman who lived in Boston Gardens, Brentford.
She told the police:

> Between three and five weeks ago, I noticed from the back
> of my house which overlooks White Horse Island, and the
> canal backwater, a man walking through the undergrowth of
> the island, carrying a sack on his back. At the time I took
> little notice, for it was morning and I was tidying up
> bedrooms. The man, who was of medium height, was

dressed in a light coloured raincoat, but he was too far off for me to describe him.

The inquest began at Southwark Coroner's Court on 10 April. In view of the fact that this was not a conventional inquest, when a known and whole corpse is examined, jurors were asked to inquire into a case 'touching certain human remains'. Many medical students attended. Evidence was initially given by those, both railway employees and the four lads, who had found the parts of the body. Donaldson said that he did not connect this discovery with the Brighton Trunk mystery. Spilsbury told the court why he thought the remains belonged to the same man. He said:

Both are the remains of men. Both show good muscular development, and the hairs in both cases are light in colour. Both are freckled, and both show complete absence of indications of previous disease and on both there is practically a complete absence of blood.

He added that the man was aged between 40 and 50, and about five feet ten inches tall.

The inquest was concluded on 18 May. An open verdict was given, meaning that no one could ascertain whether this was murder, manslaughter, accident or suicide. The coroner's concluding questions are perhaps worth considering:

Why was the parcel containing the two limbs pushed right back under the seat of the carriage so that it would not be noticeable? If we have a parcel, we do not normally push it right under the seat. It was not noticed until after the carriage cleaner found it.

Why was such meticulous care been affected in the dissecting the arms at the elbow. If the forearms had been tattooed, and anyone who knows anything about sailors knows that the forearm is a popular site for tattooing, would the removal of those forearms destroy a clue which might possibly lead to identification?

Thirdly, gentlemen, why was the head removed? Why had such care been taken to remove the stomach and intestines, leaving the kidney and the liver intact, and which are found to be perfectly healthy? Why such removal in order to prevent a pathologist from ascertaining that which might have shown the cause of death. Why was the shirt left on the trunk? Was it because there was no time to remove it?

One assessment of the crime, penned in 1952, asserted, 'The dead man ... probably belonged to the homeless and friendless class. Lacking head and hands, he was never traced. Neither was his murderer.'

The murder probably took place on 23–24 February. The body was cut up, perhaps by a slaughterman or a butcher, not necessarily anyone with medical training. A woman was probably involved; witness the female hairs on the trunk. The killing probably took place at or near Brentford, and the body parts were put in a number of containers. They were then distributed in places which would not connect them with the killer/s. So far, so good, but then there are the questions which are impossible to answer. Who was the victim, how was he killed, who killed him and why? We are never likely to know the answers with any certainty.

CHAPTER 17

Was there a Serial Strangler in Soho in 1935–1936?

I am reluctant to believe that these Soho crimes can be attributed to what is thought to be a criminal of the type of Jack the Ripper, who caused such consternation in 1888.

Prostitutes, as we have already seen in Chapters 12 and 14, are a very vulnerable class of people. Serial killers and murderers in London have preyed on them throughout the years. There was the infamous Whitechapel murderer in the East End in the late Victorian era, the poisoners Thomas Cream and George Chapman in the 1890s and 1900s, Gordon Cummins 'the blackout Ripper' in 1942, John Christie during 1943–53 and Jack the Stripper in the 1960s (out of which, only the first and last escaped the hangman). Each killed several women. There may have been a similar killer in London in the mid-1930s, too. Certainly three women, two of whom were prostitutes, were killed by the same method within a few months of each other and in the same district of London. No one was ever charged with their murders. On the other hand, several prostitutes were killed in the late nineteenth and early twentieth centuries and these were probably all by different men. We shall now examine the three killings in order.

Soho was a centre of prostitution in London. On one occasion, a policeman saw 76 girls plying their trade on one stretch of roadway near Piccadilly. It was thought that they lived like that not because they had been lured into it by a 'rotten man' but because of greed for money and expensive clothes and laziness. One writer in the 1950s considered that 'This type of crime is difficult to prevent or punish both because of the abnormal motive and of the mode of life of the victims most often chosen. ... Throughout the more civilized 1930s, however, the prowling woman killer was horribly active in London.'

Josephine Martin, 1935

Mrs Josephine Martin, whose professional name was 'French Fifi', had been born in Russia and was 41 years old in 1935. She had lived in a flat in Air Street, Piccadilly, since 1933, paying £4 a week rent. Air Street was clearly a particularly unlucky place, as Martial Lechevalier had been killed here in 1924 and in 1931 this was where Dora Lloyd met her killer. Mrs Martin was a good payer and, at the time of death, she was not in arrears (ironically she had paid up to the day of her demise). She was described as being of a kindly disposition, and was rather emotional. She had married a Henry Martin, an English waiter, in 1919. The two had separated about six months later and he emigrated to America. He had not been heard of since. Mrs Martin had employed Felicitie Plaisant, an elderly widow, who was a foreigner too, as her house maid since February 1934. She was paid £1 per week, working from noon to 11.30 pm each weekday.

She had a regular visitor, one James Orr, a 33-year-old American who had lived in England since 1932, who came around for supper on most evenings. Occasionally he gave her money and they often had sex. Yet he had gone away to Nuneaton to be cured of his drink and drug addictions and had not seen her since 1 November 1935 (she had been given £7 by him two days earlier) and did not return to London for another week.

On Sunday 3 November, Albert Mechanick, a dancing teacher of Leicester Square, and Mrs Martin's brother, visited her. He said that she complained of a little pain in her neck. She gave him some money to help him out, and had done at regular intervals previously. Yet she told him nothing about her own affairs and did not mention suicide. Detective Inspector Edward Warren noted that, three weeks previously, Mrs Martin had complained of being assaulted by a man in her flat. Apparently the man, a foreigner, had seized her by the throat, but she had not been injured and she was not afraid of him. Millicent Warren, her neighbour, had overheard her arguing with a client. Mrs Martin was heard saying, 'Come on, give me the money first, bringing me up on a fool's errand and then saying you've got no money, I've got business to do.'

Some words were then spoken in a foreign language. Shortly after the man left, Mrs Martin told her neighbour, 'He was a bilk, coming up here and yet no money. What does he take me for. Did he think I do it for love? He pushed me on the bed and I shouted out. I wasn't afraid of him.'

Her financial position was said to be shaky. Certainly she was in debt. She owed 40 guineas for one fur coat and 8 guineas for another one. These debts were being paid off at the rate of £2 a week. She also owed about £20 to another creditor. Her maid thought her total debts were just over £90. Mrs Martin's own money was apparently put in the dustbin, boxes and between the foot of her stocking and her shoe. Marie Wilson claimed to have seen between £1 and £15 in the flat in the summer of 1935. Vera Barrett thought she had seen several pounds and jewellery in the top drawer. Yet these could have been temporary windfalls, perhaps gifts from Orr.

That afternoon, Sunday 3 November, at 5 pm, Mrs Martin spoke to a friend on the telephone. In the evening, Millicent heard her having a row with a man, who had just paid her £6. It was about 9.20 pm. One John Salter had seen her with a man on Regent Street, about an hour earlier, who was aged between 25 and 30, slim, clean shaven, about five feet six and

Great Windmill Street, 2008. Author's collection

wearing a grey suit. Charles Burgess had seen her on the previous night on Windmill Street, but the man she was with was about 40, five feet ten in height and wore plus fours. Presumably he was correct about the date? Even if he was not, it is not uncommon for two witnesses to give differing descriptions.

It seems unlikely, though, that he was the killer, as she was seen alive several hours later. At 12.30 am on the following day, she was seen in the Continental Cafe and appeared happy. Over an hour later, James Weller, doorman of Mac's Club on Great Windmill Street, recalled refusing her entry, as unaccompanied women were barred. A conversation followed, perhaps for 20 minutes. Afterwards, she went to the Olde Friar's Cafe on Ham Yard, had a coffee alone, and left sometime after 2 am. There was a light in her room from in the early hours of the morning, though when Millicent Warren knocked at the door, there was no answer.

Later that morning, the maid made her a cup of tea and then went upstairs. Here she found her mistress dead, lying on her bed. There was a silk stocking, with a yellow tassel attached to her jumper, which had been passed twice around her neck and she had clearly died from asphyxiation. Charles Burton-Ball, manager of the Globe Club, which was below the flat, was called by the maid to see the body, 'Missus dead. Missus dead. Come up, come up.' He and two companions did so, and then summoned help in the form of PC John Hill, just after midday. Dr Charles Burney, the police surgeon, noted that the dead woman's left leg was bare, with the shoe and stocking removed. Her clothes had not otherwise been removed.

Spilsbury also examined the corpse and found a tattoo on the skin of her right thigh. It said 'To my Caesar for ever until I die'. This was a reference to one Caesar May, a married man, who had lived with Mrs Martin in the mid-1920s, before being deported in 1927. He had last been seen in Brussels in the previous year, but despite enquiries made to the Brussels police, he could not be traced. Spilsbury also found bruises on her abdomen, shins and neck. A thin dental plate had been removed from her mouth and it lay near her throat, in three pieces. He concluded, 'In my opinion, the deceased was forced down upon the bed where she was strangled by the right hand of an assailant. Consciousness was lost almost immediately and she was unable to struggle.' He also thought that great pressure had been used and the attacker had put his knee on her abdomen during the assault.

But although Spilsbury believed this to be a case of murder, there was an alternative view. Was suicide a possibility? Some witnesses thought she was tired of life. On 18 October, she had said, when being fined for soliciting, 'I'm fed up with this life. I've a good mind to finish with it. No money. Can't get enough to pay the fines when we get taken. I'm sick of it all.' It is also worth noting that there were no signs of disturbance in the flat, which a struggle would have caused, and there was no evidence that there had been an attacker or any other party in the room. Nothing was found under her finger nails, which, had she tried to remove a strangler's hands from around her neck, however feebly, there would have been. One harsh, but perhaps true, assessment of her, was that she was 'fat and ugly for a prostitute'. Her maid recalled that her mistress told her 'of things being none too good', being in debt to a number of creditors. James Orr wrote 'She never made a lot of money at prostitution. She worked hard, but did not get many men and could not have had much money.' Inspector Edwards wrote there were 'many reasons which point to her having committed suicide'. Yet Spilsbury's reputation, rightly or wrongly, carried all before it and it was his conclusion which was listened to.

Upon investigation, the police found that she had been seen with a young man on Regent Street on the night of her death. He was described as being tall with a fair complexion, and was wearing a mackintosh and a soft felt hat. He and Mrs Martin had taken a cab back to her flat at about 1–2 in the morning. The presumption was that he had killed her there. Unfortunately, the description given could have fitted hundreds of thousands of men in London. Furthermore, it was thought that the two people seen were Millicent Warren and her client, not Mrs Martin and hers. Mrs Martin had no regular clients and her customers included Chinese and coloured men.

Could Mrs Martin's pimp of the previous year have been to blame? It would seem not. Mrs O'Brien, a former prostitute, claimed this was a man called Shaw, who was in his late 30s, with a round face, big brown eyes and a toothbrush moustache. Yet Mrs Martin adored the man, 'I'm absolutely crazy about him. I love him and I'd do anything in the world for him and give him anything. I will kill anybody who tries to take him from me.'

Albert, her brother, was accused in an anonymous letter. This alleged that he relied on his sister for money and she had cut off his supply. 'Why was Albert so frightened when the police let him go from Vine Street? He is still terrified and he might have a good reason for his fear.' Albert had lived in England since 1902. He was apparently playing cards with his cronies on the morning of his sister's death. In any case, if he was used to receiving money from his sister, why should he kill her? If she had ceased to give him money, he may have killed her in anger.

There were various theories as to why she was killed. One was that she was the victim of gang vengeance, allegedly after having given the police information about the activity of a French crime syndicate. There were talks with the French Sureté over her activities in France. Another explanation is that she was killed for her money; perhaps £150 in total. Yet this theory, which relies on her having accumulated a tidy sum, is contradicted by her having known money worries and debts; perhaps her killer believed she did have money. Sharpe wrote, 'I believe "Fifi" was murdered by someone she took to her room on a monetary influence. Who the murderer was had not yet been established [he was writing in 1937] and may well never be.'

The inquest was held on 26 November at Westminster, being overseen by Oddie. The question of suicide was raised, but Spilsbury said that it had never been known that someone had strangled themselves with their own hand. He only knew of one textbook case in which this had been done, and that was not credited. The jury brought in a verdict of murder by person or persons unknown, such was Spilsbury's apparent authority on matters relating to forensic science.

Other names were brought up after the inquest was over. One of the first was James Metcalfe, arrested on 28 December 1935 for assaulting and robbing a prostitute. However, 'in spite of an exhaustive interrogation, he would not admit any knowledge of the affair'. One Dr Pastel of Welling was accused in an anonymous letter, but it was believed that this was written by a disgruntled former servant, and in any case he had an alibi for the night of Josephine Martin's death. Edgar Bailey, a burglar, in 1937 said that Leon Brunnick was with Mrs Martin on the night of her death. Yet Brunnick could not be traced and no prostitute had ever heard of him, so Bailey's story sounded unlikely. The police did not think he was a reliable witness, in any case, probably because he was a known criminal. Finally, in 1944, Henry Herzberg claimed Lucille Raymond/Dubois knew who the killer was. The woman, whose real name was Marie Lucie Dubois, who had several convictions, probably for prostitution, had lived at Maddox Street in London's West End. However, the premises had been bombed in the war and her current whereabouts was unknown.

It is not absolutely certain that Mrs Martin was murdered. There are grounds for believing she committed suicide.

Maddox Street, 2008. Author's collection

However, murder cannot be ruled out. The subsequent deaths of other women in Soho, however, gave added credence to the latter supposition.

Marie Jeanet Cotton, 1936

Rather more is known of the antecedents of the second victim. She was born on 30 December 1892 in the Hospital of Saint-Brieuc, Cotes du Nord, France. She had been deserted at birth and had been looked after by Mr and Madame Hamonet in Le Ruzet en Illniac, Cotes du Nord, and was brought up by them. From the age of 13, she was employed as a domestic servant at various local farms. In 1920 she went with an English family to England. In January 1924, she married one Louis Cousins in Dartford, Kent. Cousins deserted her the following year and he died in Dartford in 1929. She went to London, being employed in domestic service, chiefly in West End restaurants. In 1936 she was employed as a servant to a barrister in Savile Row, and lived in a flat in Lexington Street, Soho, paying £1 17s 6d per week for the three rooms on the second floor. This was about two minutes walk from Mrs Martin's abode. She was not a prostitute, as Sharpe observed: 'Jeanet Marie Cotton was a woman of good character and

Lexington Street, 2008. Author's collection

there was no evidence that she had ever been otherwise.' There were certainly no convictions against her for soliciting. Since 1930 she lived with one Carlo Stephano Lanza, an Italian cook at the Florence restaurant in Rupert Street, who was separated from his insane wife, and his 15-year-old son, Remo, who also worked in a kitchen. Initially they lived in rooms in Old Compton Street before moving to Lexington Street.

She was a superstitious woman. She had a number of books about fortune telling and the interpretation of dreams. She sometimes referred to signs of bad luck and carried about her a number of lucky charms. When any of these were broken, she became depressed.

At 1 pm on Thursday 16 April, Mrs Cotton finished her work at Savile Row. She went back to her flat. Lanza left for work at 4.30. Half an hour later, she was talking to Mrs Dorothy Neri, a neighbour, who was the last person known definitely to have seen her alive. Later that day a shocking discovery was made. Remo recounted the scene:

> I got home about nine o'clock and when I entered the flat I called out Mrs Cotton, but got no reply. Going into the kitchen I switched on the light and then I saw Mrs Cotton lying on the floor. I called out to her, but she did not answer and when I touched her face it was cold.

Remo called for one Alfred Gibelli, a costumier who lived upstairs (he later claimed not to have heard or seen anything unusual hitherto). After the police had arrived, Lanza senior was called and he returned from work at about 9.30.

As with Mrs Martin, she had been strangled and there was a silk stocking round her neck. According to the doctor, death had occurred at 6.30 pm or perhaps a little beforehand. In the flat were card indexes giving the names and addresses of five managers of cinemas in the Midlands and the north of England. They were questioned and all claimed to know nothing of her.

Twenty detectives were initially put on the case. Three hours were spent in examining the dead woman's room. The door of the flat was removed for scientific examination, for bloodstains

Rupert Street, 2008. Author's collection

were allegedly found on it. Unfortunately the only fingerprint that could be found in the flat was that of PC Rough. Chief Inspector Sharpe was the officer in charge. On the Monday following her death, the police issued a statement, asking for information, and distributed a copy of her photograph. Anyone wanting information was requested to contact the Commissioner at Scotland Yard.

Money was not the motive for this murder. Police found £14 in notes and silver in an open cupboard in the room in which the body was found. Nor had she been subjected to a sexual assault. Sharpe dismissed there being a link between her death and that of 'Red' Max Kassel, a notorious figure in the underworld, whose corpse had been recently discovered near St Albans, but who may have been killed in Soho. It was reputed that Mrs Cotton had been involved in the vice trade and her murder was in order to silence her. 'Well this is base libel', wrote Sharpe. Another senior detective on the case, Chief Inspector Hambrooke, said that the murder 'cannot be associated with the usual class of murder'. Unfortunately, he did not write about the case in his memoirs.

It was discovered that Mrs Cotton had visited her old family, the Hamonets, in 1935. The Sureté confirmed this, but added that she was not 'known to the police' in that country. A friend in France did tell the police that a man there had been known to threaten her with violence. He was questioned and ruled out.

Initially, there were two men the police wished to locate for questioning. One was her estranged husband, who was then not thought to be deceased. The other was one Harry Cohen, who allegedly paid occasionally visits to her flat. Mrs Neri said that Mrs Cotton was very much afraid of one man, 'a Jew man' who had demanded money from her and that she was in love with another man. This was Dennis from Canada, her 'sweetheart', though he was never traced. Apparently, she had arranged with her friend to drop a utensil in order to warn her if her enemy had arrived. She added that, on the evening of 14 April, she and Mrs Cotton had gone out together and left a note outside the door, with the following written on the envelope, 'Mr Cohen. Shall not be long. Gone to Marlborough Street.' On their return, they found the note was intact. Efforts had been made to locate Cohen, but as the coroner, Oddie noted, 'Well, we have hunted all over London trying to find out who this man Cohen is. There are thousands of them and it is a pretty hopeless task.' Could this Mr Cohen have been the Harry Cohen who was released from jail in the autumn of 1934? It was presumably not Sidney Cohen, a costumier, who lived in Hendon and had a shop in the West End, whom Mrs Cotton asked for the whereabouts of James Allan Hall.

Hall was a 28-year-old clerk, paid £3 a week, who was separated from his wife, and who had been a neighbour of Mrs Cotton. Hall had been violent to his estranged wife during the marriage ('She was frequently assaulted'). In 1935 and early 1936 he lived in one of the rooms in Lexington Street. He was homosexual and often invited men back to the flat, including a Scotsman called Donald Ross and several soldiers. Between them, they had damaged a mattress belonging to Mrs Cotton and the latter wanted compensation for this, amounting to £3. He had left Lexington Street at the end of January, moving to lodgings in Craven Street, where he was having problems with paying the rent. Hall and Mrs Cotton had been in correspondence about the mattress and she had threatened

Craven Street, 2008. Author's collection

him with a court proceeding. The two had arranged to meet
on the day before the murder, but it appears they did not do
so. Therefore, he had a motive of a kind and did not have an
alibi for the evening of 16 April, claiming he spent it in
cinemas and pubs in Charing Cross Road, but 'it is impossible
to verify in every detail the truth of what he says'. He 'created
a most unfavourable impression in the minds of the jury'. Yet
there was no evidence that he had entered the flat that evening
and he had only a minor grievance against Mrs Cotton. Thus
he was ruled out.

Another suspect was Lanza. He had been born in Italy in
1892, came to England in 1912 and briefly served in the army
1918–1919. He married in 1920 and had two children.
According to Neri, he and Mrs Cotton had 'frequent quarrels'
and 'did not get on well together'. Yet she had seen no sign of
physical violence. Josephine Pouliquen from Boulogne, a
friend of the deceased, told the police 'I feel certain my friend
was murdered by Mr Lanza, he is a brute and often kicked
Madame Cotton.' As he was at work at the time of the murder
he must presumably be ruled out, though as Rupert Street is
only a couple of minutes away from Lexington Street, he could

have just popped out, committed the deed and returned.

Then there were lesser suspects. A man in a prison cell who had a picture of Mrs Cotton with him, and a man seen in Regent Street, who appeared to have recently been in a fight, were both suspected. Sharpe thought that none of these men were guilty, writing that many other men were questioned and 'Against one of these persons – to whom I have not previously referred [i.e. not Cohen, Lanza or Hall] – there was a strong suspicion'. Sharpe was convinced that he had spoken to this unnamed man in the course of his investigation. It was 'someone she knew'. Yet not even in the police file is this man mentioned, though some pages are still closed and names blacked out, so perhaps Sharpe's suspect is mentioned there? Presumably so, as Sharpe noted there was a dossier at the Yard which 'tells more than I possibly can'.

Sharpe concluded:

> We could not get enough evidence to take any action, although it was not through lack of trying. The case is still an unsolved murder mystery, but at the same time the investigation remains and will remain – open. Unless something fresh turns up it is not likely that the murderer of Jeanette Marie Cotton will be brought to trial.

Motive was unclear, since it was neither money nor sexual assault. The police thought that 'It is clear that the crime was committed by some person who knew the woman and had been to the place before.' She had no known male friends and did not go to pubs. The communal door to the flats was locked after six. Either she let someone in whom she trusted or perhaps one of Neri's clients killed her. A man called Alban was one of her regular clients and he was with her after half past six, though the murder probably was committed before then. There is no obvious reason for him to have killed her. Only Hall had any known animosity against her and it seems unlikely she would have let him in; Lanza had an alibi, so both seem unlikely.

Leah Hinds/Smith, 1936

Mrs Smith was the youngest of these victims, aged about 23 or 24 on death in 1936. She was born in the East Ham Infirmary in 1912 and was known as 'Stilts Leah', on account of her wearing high heels, and 'Dutch Leah'. She was illegitimate, being the daughter of Kathleen Hinds and an engineer. She had been a difficult girl when young and lived with her grandmother, as her mother had tried to help her but had failed. She had left home whilst in her teens and had lived with a variety of men, one being a coloured man. This was Jim Rich, an entertainer, in 1930–2, who was apparently only interested in her for her money. Three other men who had made money from her were in prison in 1936. She had also had a baby in 1931 (who was soon adopted by someone else) and had married, in June 1933, Robert Thomas Smith, a Margate waiter. However, in August 1934 she had left him.

Other men in her life were William Sullivan, John Sutton, Alfred an Italian and George a Frenchman. As might be imagined, she moved address often, living in Bloomsbury High Street in 1935–6. At the beginning of April 1936, she met one Stanley King, born in Aldershot in 1912, the son of a soldier. He

Old Compton Street, 2008. Author's collection

had come to London in 1931 and had worked in restaurants and nightclubs. Initially he had been a waiter, but by 1936 did conjuring tricks for a living. It was a seedy world in which he lived. One club he worked in was in Old Compton Street and was 'a low class place and generally frequented by moral perverts and undesirables'. Leah was in love with him and, as a friend declared, 'She didn't intend to give him up as he had been very good to her and she loved him very much.' Yet King, who initially believed Leah was a waitress, when he discovered her profession was unhappy about it and wanted her to cease. They took rooms in Little Pulteney Street, but soon moved.

By early May 1936, they were living in a flat on the second floor at Old Compton Street, a dilapidated property. King wanted to move again, in the hope that she might discard her old ways, but there was little chance of that. There were arguments between them and King, who worked in the evenings, was unable to supervise her then, at her most active time and she brought men home, as she always had. It was Leah who had the only key between them and so he could not surprise her by arriving unannounced.

She was a well-known figure in the West End and often was seen in Cambridge Circus. Mrs Hinds was well known to the police, too. As the police report declared, she was 'a low type of prostitute and a habitué of low class clubs in the Soho district'. At the time of her death she had eight convictions for soliciting.

On the evening Friday 8 May, Leah had been with several clients. Late that night she was seen on Old Compton Road, talking to Joan Maymar and another woman. It was about half past eleven. A Greek pestered Leah, who refused him. He had been a client of hers, but only paid her half of the 10s promised in advance of the transaction. At a quarter to midnight, Leah left her friends, saying 'I must try and get some money, I'm fed up, I haven't been off tonight yet and there is no money coming in.' Leah and Joan walked down Old Compton Street and parted outside the Palace Theatre just before midnight.

Just after midnight on Saturday 9 May, Emilio Piantino, the hall porter of the London Casino Restaurant, Old Compton

Street, saw her with a man. He stated, 'I was in the hall looking out into the street when I saw Leah Hinds with a man on the opposite side of the road walking towards Wardour Street. The man was on the inside of the pavement away from me and I do not think I would know him again.' Yet he later said that the man was of fair complexion, slim, clean shaven and with thinning hair. He wore a dark raincoat but, eccentrically enough, was hatless. At half past twelve, two girls saw the two of them enter her flat. One of the women was Nellie Few, who had known Leah for six years. Lily Joyce was the other and she recalled Leah saying 'if you can't get it in the day, you must get it at night'. The man they saw was probably the same man seen by Piantino, described as being aged about 30, five feet eight tall, with long hair and a slouching gait. Police thought that such a bohemian character must be either a foreigner or, worse, an artist. He was not a known criminal. She was never seen alive again.

Later that morning, King called on her as arranged. He had tried several times from 4 am. At 8.45 am he rang again, but no one answered. After two more attempts to gain her attention, and after he heard her puppy whining within, he gave up. He left and soon found himself in a nearby restaurant where he met James Adams of no fixed abode, a pal from the previous evening. The two went to the flat and Adams broke the door down. The two men soon left and sought a policeman. PC John Davidson was found and Adams said, 'Oh constable, will you come along, I think a girl has been murdered. I have just broken into the flat and I saw her on the bed. Her head was covered with blood. I think her throat is cut. This poor little dog was with her.'

The police investigation was quick to take effect and, as before, Sharpe was in charge. First there was an examination of the scene of the crime. The victim was still partially dressed, though her stockings had been rolled down, probably by the woman herself, and she was lying on the bed, probably ready for her client. She had been strangled, by means of a thin wire, but her face had also been battered and there were bruises on the lower jaw and lower lip. The blows had been first, then the strangulation. She had probably met her death at about 12.55

am; possibly a little later, but not after 3 am. She had not been sexually assaulted. This savage attack led some to believe the attacker was 'a dangerous homicidal maniac'.

Spilsbury examined her. He said that the head injuries were caused by a blunt instrument, such as the flat iron found in the flat. Any one of these several injuries would have rendered her unconscious. Yet it was the electric light wire around her throat which had caused death.

Elsewhere, her handbag was found on the floor, but there was only two pence there. Sharpe concluded 'Robbery was the most likely motive for this murder, for Leah was known to have had money in her bag that night.' Another clue was found on the edge of the wooden mantelpiece in the room. This was a fingerprint, which was shown not to be of anyone who normally had access to the room. That part of the mantelpiece with the incriminating mark was sawn off and carried away to the laboratory. However, the print did not match any of those in the police files. There were also fingerprints of Leah and King, as expected.

Another clue was a set of seaman's papers. These were of a James Rose, a sailor who had recently visited her, and had lost them. He was soon tracked down and told the police that he had seen her a few days prior to the murder and had not returned for the papers because he could not remember where she lived. He could be proved to have been aboard ship at Margate on the night of the murder, so he was ruled out.

It was thought that six men had seen Mrs Hinds on her last evening. They were asked to report to the police, but unsurprisingly, none did. It was also rumoured that she had a rich Chinaman as a client. He insisted that she wore red stockings, even in public places, which she had agreed to. Mr Smith was questioned, but he had not seen her since she left him two years before. Some men who had previously been seen with her had left their usual haunts.

The police made a list of men who had been convicted of assaulting prostitutes in London in the past 18 months. These numbered 103. Some did not live in London. These men included Herbert Haynes of Hoddesdon, Gerald Barnes of Hertford, and George Brown, an undergraduate of Magdalene

Magdalene College, Cambridge. Author's collection

College, Cambridge. These men looked like the man seen with Leah. Yet all had alibis; Brown being at his college on the night of the murder for instance.

There was one man who does not seem to have been considered as a suspect, though perhaps he should have been. This was Captain Edward Broughton Smythe of the Essex Regiment, aged 35 in 1936. Although he bore an excellent character (he had served on the North West Frontier in 1930–1 and had gained medals there), he had recently retired due to chronic alcoholism and was undergoing treatment by Dr Leonard Brown of Harley Street. He also had no permanent address, but in 1936 was living in a hotel in Sidcup, Kent.

He deserves consideration as a suspect because in late May 1936, he went to a young woman's flat in Gerrard Street, Soho, in the early hours of the morning. He put his hands around one Miss Bedford's neck, pushed her backwards and said he would like to strangle her, though he later denied this. He later gripped her around the throat and Miss Bedford's screams aroused her companion, Phyllis Thompson, who rushed to her aid. There is no doubt that he attempted to

Gerrard Street, 2008. Author's collection

strangle her, as fingernail marks were found around her neck, and Miss Bedford claimed that he was laughing whilst he had her by the throat. Smythe was dealt with leniently, being bound over to keep the peace and had to pay costs. One wonders whether he may have committed more serious crimes where his victim was alone, or whether he was copying aspects of the Soho murders. After all, there were numerous similarities. Whatever the case, Smythe rejoined his old regiment with the outbreak of war in 1939 and saw active service again, going onto the army reserve list in 1942.

Extensive searches were carried out in the vicinity of Soho shortly after the discovery of the crime. Lodging houses and boarding houses were examined. Any discarded clothes were also investigated as the killer might have thrown away any bloodstained clothes. Second-hand clothing shops were told to keep a look out for such. Some women came forward with what little they knew and were assured police protection as the number of officers in the district was increased. It was found that many such women lived in danger of threats of violence. As Sharpe noted, 'Soho was turned upside down'. Yet he was pessimistic about the outcome, writing, 'with so little to go on we were pretty well doomed to failure from the word "go"'.

It seems certain that a stranger killed her. Joan said 'Leah Hinds has not had at any time complained to me of being frightened of any person or anyone ill treating her'. Her mother, who saw her a few days before her death, recalled, 'She seemed perfectly happy and did not complain of being afraid of any person.' The motive was probably the little money she had on her person, the police stating 'It is reasonable to assume that robbery was the motive.' After all, the handbag was empty and only two pence could be found in the room. The possibility of revenge by a former pimp was not seen as serious because there was no evidence of any quarrels or disorder in the room. The police conclusion was as follows:

> The circumstances of the case rather indicate that her assailant was a chance acquaintance who accompanied her home for the purpose of robbery. The ferocity with which he attacked the unfortunate girl suggests he is a dangerous homicidal man.

George Killik, a Danish ex-jockey and an alleged diviner with mysterious powers of visions, was shown photographs of the deceased by a newspaper. He claimed: 'I see another girl who is in danger of her life.' He thought the killer was a poor man, though once rich, who was thin, with large hands and dressed shabbily. Although not a London resident, he occasionally visited the city.

Leah's estranged husband reported to the police as soon as he knew of the murder. He was resident in Margate and had a strong alibi for the night of the murder as he was with friends and had been seen by tradesmen on the following morning. King, too, can probably be eliminated as a suspect as he was at a nightclub on Little Denmark Street from 11.15 pm to 3.30 am. In any case, he seems to have been on excellent terms with her, despite disliking her calling.

Soho and the girls and women who worked the streets became increasingly frightened after this murder. Sharpe wrote 'This was Soho's fourth murder within six months, the papers were talking of a new Jack the Ripper'. This was despite the fact that the Ripper's victims had their throats cut and were mutilated.

Although Mrs Cotton's inquest had begun on 21 April, it was adjourned and the inquests on both her and Mrs Hinds were concluded at Westminster Coroners' Court on 9 June. Neither was conclusive. Both were cases of murder and had been committed by an unknown killer. No one was ever convicted of either crime, nor that of Mrs Martin in the previous year.

It is tempting to conclude that a serial strangler was at work here. After all, the women all lived within a short distance at each other and were all killed within six months. All were strangled. Two were prostitutes. All the murders occurred indoors. The press certainly thought this was a series, but it was uncertain whether any of the women knew one another. Mrs Hind's mother said, 'So far as I know, she was not acquainted with the victims of the previous murders.' On the other hand, some street women, friends of Mrs Hinds, said that she knew the other two victims. Apparently 'Rightly or wrongly, rumour attributed them to some known hand, especially if that hand had already struck more than once.' It was said, 'While some of Scotland Yard's chiefs are inclined to think that the affairs are in no way related, it is pointed out that the possibility of one man being responsible for them all cannot be ruled out.' It was not only the press which thought so, because Detective Inspector Edwards, who had investigated the Mrs Martin case, thought that the papers of this case 'might be of assistance in the cases of Jeanett Cousins and Constance May Smith alias Leah Hinds at present under investigation'.

In the case of Leah, it was concluded, 'There is nothing to show, however, that there is a connection between any of these cases'. Retired and active senior detectives agreed. Ex-Chief Inspector Walter Dew wrote in a newspaper article that such killings occurred periodically among women 'of a Bohemian character [who] invite strange men sometimes to their rooms or flats' and were not part of a series. He thought the killers were ill-tempered men who attacked their victims 'without any or little provocation'. He thought that the police would be sure to catch the guilty men and that, if not, they might know who was responsible but lack the evidence needed to convict.

Similarly, Sharpe wrote as follows:

> The murders of French Fifi and Jeannette Cousins remaining unsolved drove us to redouble our efforts to solve the further crime of Soho, but it is unlikely it ever will be solved. I don't think there was any connection between those killings or that they were in any way connected with any vice ring or other organisation. In my opinion: French Fifi was murdered for the money in her flat by someone she had picked up, and Leah Hinds for the same reason. Jeanette Cousins was killed by someone she knew and the motive was one which I believe I know but which I think it best not to mention.

The culprits were never found. Sharpe wrote: 'Despite the most exhaustive enquiries no evidence could be found upon which even suspicion could be attached to any known person and it is unlikely that the crime will ever be solved.'

Sharpe was best placed to know about these crimes. Therefore, his verdict should hold good, unless other evidence comes to light. At time of writing, the police files on the two latter murders are still partially closed (despite the fact that over seven decades have passed) and until they are fully opened, we are no nearer the truth than the public were in 1936. The only consolation was that, after the death of Leah, there were no more known unsolved killings in this part of London for the rest of the decade.

CHAPTER 18

Murder in Southall, 1938

Some people deserve all they get

The reader will have noticed that a number of the characters featured in this book, whether as victims, suspects or witnesses, were immigrants from overseas – from France, Russia, Lithuania, Italy, Africa and India. Capital cities attract migrants, and whilst the level in London was by no means comparable to that in the later twentieth century and beyond, their numbers in the London of the 1920s and 1930s were not insignificant either. However, as they had for centuries, people came there from all over the British Isles, too, and usually they were seeking work.

One such man was Frederick Henry Priddle, who was born in Thomastown, Glamorgan, in 1913. His father was a coal miner. The depression of the 1930s had badly affected employment in many parts of Britain, and these included the coal-mining districts of Wales. Many young men and women left Wales in the 1930s and looked for employment in London, as new industries were being set up in and around the capital.

Priddle first arrived in London as part of the government's transfer scheme and undertook training in acetylene welding at Park Royal, West London. From 1933 to 1936 he worked at Woolf's Rubber factory in Cricklewood, and then in Hayes. Towards the end of 1936 he fell ill and returned to his home town, where, after recovering, he worked in a colliery for a few months. Bad health struck again, and he decided to return to London. From April 1937, he was employed by L Clarke & Co., engineers and welders of Acme Works, Pluckington Place, Southall. His employers described him as 'a conscientious and capable workman'.

Priddle was an inoffensive figure, described as being a 'very quiet and reserved young man, who did not mix with a lot of people, but kept to the company of a few childhood friends'.

It seems that there were several hundred Welsh in Southall in the later 1930s. He was a teetotaller and rarely went out. When he lived in Wales, he was interested in first aid and was a member of the St John's Ambulance Brigade. In 1934 he had become engaged to a Welsh girl, Miss Eunice Wiggins, who had been born in Pontypridd, Glamorgan, in 1911. They had been friends since 1931. She had lived in Southall since February 1937, being her widowed brother's housekeeper. Priddle often spent his evenings with her, going to one of the four cinemas in the town, or stayed in with her and her brother. Although the young couple had made no fixed plans, now Priddle had a steady job they were hoping to marry before long.

On 31 December 1937, they went to the house of a fellow Welshman in Portland Road, Southall. A New Year's party was being held and there were party games. Everyone seemed to have a good time. Although Priddle was a teetotaller, he was reported as drinking three glasses of wine. Miss Wiggins had her fortune told by another guest. She later recalled, 'I was going to hear of a broken engagement' and that 'I should hear of an illness and be sent for quickly to someone's bedside'.

Gordon Road, Southall, 2005. Author's collection

None of these predictions are difficult to make, as vague as they are. Unfortunately, they came true rather more quickly than anyone would have expected. At the time, Miss Wiggins only thought 'I had the impression that it was meant to refer to an elderly person living a long way away.'

A sober Priddle and his fiancée left the party at 12.35 in the morning. He escorted her to where she lived and then went down South Road and the Green. He stopped off at the coffee bar on Station Road, before arriving at his lodgings in the quiet back street that was Gordon Road. Unlocking the front door, Priddle went into the living room. It was in darkness, but he could see a man by the fireplace. He was 'wearing a light coat and a cap and was about 5 foot 8 inches'. Priddle was then kicked in the stomach and received a stab wound. He fell unconscious. His next memory was of staggering outside and reaching the garden gate.

It was at 1.30 that his landlord, David Walker, aged 51, who found him there. Walker had been awoken by the loud groans he had heard. Looking out of the window, Walker saw the collapsed Priddle and, at his wife's urgings, rushed downstairs. Once there, he said to his tenant, 'Come on, old son, what is the matter with you?' Then he noticed that blood was flowing from Priddle's chest, where he had been stabbed. Walker called his wife down.

The two helped him inside their house and called for the police and for an ambulance to take him to the local hospital. Apart from the chest wound, which was four inches deep, there was another stab wound to the head, too. The weapon which inflicted both of these was probably a narrow-bladed dagger, such as a stiletto. No weapon was found.

Once in hospital, the police kept a watch at his bedside. Priddle did regain consciousness briefly and was able to give his confused account of the assault (as noted above). There were no witnesses and no one in that quiet back street had seen anyone acting oddly.

It was unclear what the motive was. A few items, it was true, were missing from the room where Priddle had been stabbed. These were two boxes of matches, 8s 6d from the mantelpiece, and an electric light bulb had been removed. Hardly enough to provide a motive for murder. The police theory was that two homeless men had been in the locality and had got into the house seeking warmth, shelter and food. They would enter a house, make themselves comfortable, put coals on the fire and heat up some food. Anything valuable would be taken. The police made enquiries about these men.

Events took a tragic turn in the early morning of 14 January when Priddle died in hospital. There had been hopes that he might recover, but the loss of blood and the onset of pneumonia proved fatal. Miss Wiggins and Priddle's mother were with him when he died. His father had seen his injured son, but was not there at his deathbed, because he had to return to work. Although recalled, he did not arrive before his son died.

This was now a case of murder and the police had lost their only witness to the attack. Divisional Detective Inspector Baker and his men investigating the case redoubled their efforts. The two homeless men were found and questioned, but nothing conclusive emerged. They had to be released due to lack of witnesses and evidence. Other witnesses claimed that a tall dark man had been seen running from the scene of the crime and that a motor car had been heard in the vicinity of the house, too.

The inquest was convened at St John's Hall on 17 January. It was very short. Priddle's uncle identified the corpse and the inquest was then adjourned until 8 February, in order to give the police more time to conduct their investigation. Dr Broadridge, the police surgeon, carried out a post mortem on the body and hoped to be able to find a particle of the murder weapon. He was unable to do so. Reginald Kemp, the coroner for West Middlesex, announced at the concluding part of the inquest that the police 'had an extraordinarily difficult task before them because there is so little for them to go on'. Miss Wiggins and Mr Walker thought that Priddle had no enemies and knew of no reason why anyone would have wanted to kill him. Frank Mortimer, proprietor of the coffee stall which Priddle had stopped at on his way back home on the fatal morning, recalled Priddle being his usual self: quiet, but cheerful. He said that Priddle hoped to catch a bus, but

Mortimer told him that none were running at that time. Priddle had answered him 'Allright, I'll have to hoof it then.' Mr Walker thought that Priddle had been attacked on the way home, yet Priddle's testimony contradicted this theory, for he had said he was attacked only when he was inside the house. Frustratingly, the inquest could only end in one way – that Priddle had been killed by person or persons unknown.

There was much local sympathy for the family of the dead man, who were numerous and not well off. A total of 156 people from neighbouring streets sent £4 7s 3d to the Priddle family. His workmates and employers also gave the family a collection, and sent a wreath. The funeral was in Wales on 19 January. His family wrote to their son's friends in Southall to express their thanks at their kindness and generosity.

The police investigation continued, but little concrete was discovered. A number of suspects emerged. One was Walker himself, who incidentally continued to live in the same house until the late 1970s. Yet Priddle had been asked about his landlord, and refuted this possibility. One Edward Hooper, a Scot and an army deserter, had a track record of breaking into houses for shelter. However, it could be shown that he had an alibi for the time of the assault on Priddle. He was illegally entering St Luke's Vicarage in Hammersmith. Likewise, Llewellyn Davis, a well-known burglar, was another suspect, but again he had an alibi for the night of the crime.

Others wrote to the police about lodgers and acquaintances who acted oddly at the time. People who had blood on their clothes were reported, for instance. A man who was heard commenting on the case, 'Some people deserve all they get', was reported. A local newsagent recalled being asked by a man, just after the deed, who lived in another part of London whether he could be sent local newspapers. A Mr Knight from Salisbury told the police that a man whom he had known in Lewisham possessed a stiletto. William Triffit, a prisoner, spoke about an acquaintance who was a burglar and carried a stiletto, but this turned out to be an invention.

The mystery remained unsolved. It would seem that Priddle was very unfortunate in being in the wrong place at the wrong time, that his assailant/s did not attack him through any personal motive, but because he interrupted their illegal activities and they wanted to avoid being arrested. The lack of clues and witnesses hampered any successful investigation. The police concluded:

> the person who committed this murder was a paltry thief, in need of warmth and shelter, and by the ferocity of his assault upon the unfortunate man, is in all probability, youthful and inexperienced in crime.

Baker concluded the case by writing in his official report, on 5 October 1938:

> Despite every possible enquiry and constant touch being kept with persons likely to be able to assist us in this difficult case, no progress has been made. In the event of any useful information coming to hand, it will at once be acted upon and a further report submitted.

Death in Hyde Park, 1938

The man struck me for nothing at all.

T his last case of murder is one of the most mysterious in this book. This is not only because the murderer escaped unscathed – all the killers whose crimes have been catalogued here did – but because there is so little information about it. There is no police file surviving for the case, unlike the majority of murders chronicled here. Furthermore, both the national and the local press only contained the scantiest details. Although there were many clues in the case of Vera Page, there were none in this and a featureless murder is the most difficult to solve. As Sherlock Holmes said in *A Study in Scarlet*, 'The most commonplace crime is the most mysterious, because it presents no new or special features from which deductions can be drawn.' The few known facts are as follows.

Cecil Johnson, an osteopath, and his friend, Thomas Barnwell, aged 26, a commissionaire, who once served as a corporal in the Irish Guards, shared a flat at Holbein House, Pimlico Road, in Chelsea. The two men had known each other since the autumn of 1936. This was probably when the regiment was stationed at the Wellington Barracks in London (they had not been overseas since 1924). The flat belonged to Johnson, but he allowed his friend to stay there since Barnwell left the army in February 1938, after serving in Egypt, where his regiment had been posted in November of the previous year. Initially this was meant to be until Barnwell found a new job, but he was still there in May of that year. Johnson's business premises were at Evelyn Mansions, Carlisle Place, Victoria.

On the evening of Sunday 15 May, the two men went out at about 8.30, and spent the next hour and a half in public houses, the last one being on Edgware Road. They left at ten and headed

The Serpentine Road and Band Stand, Hyde Park. Author's collection

for home. They were travelling south across Hyde Park on foot, probably on Broad Walk, and had just turned into the path which led to the Serpentine. Johnson later recalled that two men who they did not know passed them by. Without any provocation, or any words passing between them, one of the strangers apparently hit Barnwell on the face. Barnwell retaliated and a scuffle followed. Johnson joined in. The two men rushed off and Barnwell followed them. Johnson later recalled:

> When I got up to them a second time Barnwell was standing alone. The two men had walked away. Barnwell was holding his side. He thought he had been kicked. I did not know either of the two men. Barnwell said he did not know them.

Barnwell and Johnson staggered to Marble Arch Gate and hailed a taxi cab on Park Lane. They went to St George's Hospital, on Grovsenor Lane, and about a mile from the park, arriving at 10.40. Dr A C Grey found that Barnwell had been stabbed in the groin by a sharp instrument. He was operated upon two hours after admission – he could not have been operated on sooner because he was in a state of shock. Unfortunately, peritonitis developed and there were intestinal obstructions.

Barnwell was questioned on 17 May by Divisional Detective Inspector Sydney Kidd. He told the detective:

> I was walking across the meeting ground. The man struck me for nothing at all. There were two men, both about 26 to 30. As far as I know I have never seen them before, and I don't think I would know them again. I don't know if they were Guardsmen, but they were of that type. I was not under the influence of drink.

Johnson also asked if he could describe their attackers, but he said, 'I might, but I don't say for certain. I could not describe them.'

On the same day, a police message was sent out asking for information. It read:

> At about 10.20 pm on Sunday night a man, aged 26, height 6ft., 4 in., was stabbed in the stomach during an affray at the meeting ground, Hyde Park, near Broad Walk. He was escorted to Marble Arch Gate and taken by taxicab to hospital, where he is critically ill. Anyone who saw the

Marble Arch. Author's collection

incident and who can give any information, please ring
Whitehall 1212 or any police station.

Clearly the man who helped Barnwell was Johnson.

Despite an improvement in his condition, on 24 May
Barnwell died. According to Dr John Taylor, a pathologist at
the hospital, heart failure was the cause of death, due to
peritonitis flowing from the wound in the abdominal wall of
the left groin.

The inquest was held at Westminster on 27 May.
Christopher Stephen Barnwell, the dead man's brother, and a
commissionaire at Richmond Hill Hotel, was present and
merely stated that his brother had been in the Guards until
February of that year. Oddie, the coroner, announced at its
conclusion:

> It is a very strange story. Without a word of provocation one
> of these unknown strangers struck the deceased. Quite
> obviously it is a case of murder. All homicide is considered
> to be murder until the contrary is proved. It was a malicious
> attack, and has resulted in this young man's death.

There is no obvious reason why Barnwell was killed. As no
one else witnessed the murder, it is tempting to suggest that
Johnson killed him, but given his and Barnwell's stories were
the same, this would seem to have been ruled out.
Furthermore, had Johnson attacked his erstwhile friend, why
would he help him to hospital where he might recover and
incriminate him? No, it was one of the two men they met who
was guilty. Since Barnwell did not recognize his attackers, he
was clearly unknown to them, so this was not a settling of a
grudge. Therefore, it would seem that this was a spur of the
moment killing, carried out by a young man who had a knife
and used it during the second phase of the scuffle. The killer
must have been in an angry mood when he and his companion
met Johnson and Barnwell. It was the latter's misfortune to
chase after his assailant, not realizing the risk he was running.
One possibility is that Barnwell and Johnson were lovers (they
were certainly on friendly terms) and were showing signs of

affection in public, and that this triggered violence on the part of the other two men. Barnwell and Johnson could not have alluded to this to the authorities for their activity would then have been classified as immoral (and illegal) behaviour. Whether or not this was the case is, of course, another question.

Conclusion

These 20 London murders which occurred in the years between the two world wars are all those which were unsolved in this period. However, we should note that three may not have been murders at all – those of Edith Emms, Kusel Behr and Josephine Martin. This is a very small number of unsolved murders, which work out at approximately one per year.

Of these murders, assuming all were murders, nine were of men, one was of a child and ten were women (four of these being prostitutes). Strangulation was the most common method, accounting for six murders, with bludgeoning accounting for another four. Three were shot and another three were stabbed. One victim was electrocuted, another was poisoned and the method of death for two are unknown. For most of these crimes the motive is unknown, though four were concerned with money, two were political and one was motivated by sexual perversion. Apart from Behr, all the victims were of working-class or occasionally lower middle-class origin.

Some of these killings, perhaps the majority, were murders by strangers, which made them all the more difficult to solve. It is probable that the death of Behr and the murder of Vera Page were both the responsibility of someone who knew the victim/s fairly well. Except in the case of poisoning, the killers were almost certainly all male – and may have been in that too, as poison is not exclusively used by women. All managed to commit their crimes without having any inconvenient witnesses around and managed to avoid leaving any damning clues. Although the police had their suspicions about some men, such as Field in the Norah Upchurch case and Philpotts in the Emberton one, there was never enough evidence to convict them, and in the latter case, not enough even to bring him to trial.

The majority of these crimes took place in west London, especially in the district around Leicester Square. Only one occurred in the East End and only five in south London, with one in Croydon, and there were only two in north London. Perhaps one reason behind this is that vice was more fashionable an industry in the West End at that time than in the East End (the Ripper's victims in the Victorian age were all from the East End, of course).

The killers escaped the penalty of their actions in these cases, leaving behind them corpses and unanswered questions. They remain as mysterious today as they did then. The guilty walked free and their secrets died with them. Perhaps some of their descendants will read this book, completely unaware that it was their ancestor who was an undiscovered killer.

Bibliography

Primary Sources

National Archives
Metropolitan Police Files: MEPO3/268b (Buxton), 852 (Emms), 855 (Behr), 861 (Duff and Sidneys), 887 (Emberton), 1606 (Lechevalier), 1611 (Goodall), 1623a (Creed), 1648 (East), 1609 (Upchurch), 1671 (Page), 1672 (Lloyd), 1698 (Brentford/Waterloo corpse), 1702 (Martin), 1706 (Cousins), 1707 (Leah), 2190 (Priddle)
Principal Division of the Family: Will of Kusel Behr, 1926; Wills of Violet and Vera Sidney, 1929

Newspapers Consulted
Acton Gazette, 1920
Illustrated Police News, 1920, 1921, 1926, 1931, 1932, 1935, 1936
Kensington News, 1931–2
Kentish Mercury, 1929
Middlesex Independent, 1935
Southall–Norwood Gazette, 1926, 1938
Thomson's Weekly News, 1936
The Times, 1920–4, 1926, 1929, 1931–2, 1935–6, 1938
West London Observer, 1921
Westminster and Pimlico News, 1938

Other Printed Sources
G Cornish, *Cornish of the Yard* (1935)
T Divall, *Scoundrels and Scallywags* (1929)
Kensington North Electoral Registers, 1918–47
A F Neil, *40 Years of Manhunting* (1932)
S I Oddie, *Inquest* (1941)
F D Sharpe, *Sharpe of the Flying Squad* (1938)
B Thomson, *The Story of Scotland Yard* (1935)
A Thorp, *Calling Scotland Yard* (1954)
E Waugh, *Brideshead Revisited* (1945)
E Waugh, *Diaries* (1976)
F Wensley, *Detective Days* (1931)

Oral Reminiscences
William Bignell

Electronic Sources
Ancestry.com
Timesonline

Secondary Sources
H L Adam, *Murder by Persons Unknown* (1931)
D G Browne and E V Tulloch, *Sir Bernard Spilsbury: His Life and Crimes* (1951)
The Chap Manifesto (2001)
N Connell, *Walter Dew: The Man Who Caught Crippen* (2005)
T A Critchley, *The Police in England and Wales* (1968)
C Emsley, *The English Police* (1991)
J G Hall and G D Smith, *The Croydon Arsenic Mystery* (1999)
S Inswood, *A History of London* (1998)
J D Oates, *Foul Deeds and Suspicious Deaths in Ealing* (2006)
J D Oates, *Foul Deeds and Suspicious Deaths in Lewisham and Deptford* (2007)
J D Oates, *Unsolved Murders in Victorian and Edwardian London* (2007)
Oxford Dictionary of National Biography (2004)
A Rose, *Lethal Witness* (2007)
C J S Thompson, *Poison and Poisoners* (1993)
J White, *London in the Twentieth Century* (2000)
J R Whitbread, *The Railway Policeman* (1961)

Index